HANDBOOK

CONCEPT & DESIGN

JEAN-BENOÎT LÉVY

INTRODUCTION

PROF. CLAUDE VERDAN

TEXTS

AARON MARCUS

ERIK ADIGARD

JEAN-BENOÎT LÉVY

EDITING

MAURICE BASSAN

PUBLICATION

LARS MÜLLER

THANKS

First, my special thanks to Claudia Dallendörfer, my partner in life and in work who helped me with her trust and patience to realize this book. She has depicted and photographed an important and essential amount of the images printed here. Somehow, this is also her book.

The quality of this book has been enhanced thanks to the help of Francesco Panese, with texts from Prof. Claude Verdan, Aaron Marcus, Erik Adigard. The editing is by Maurice Bassan. Illustration from Niklaus Heeb. Images from Claudia Dallendörfer and others who are credited with their pictures.

I am sending also my visual thanks to all of the graphic designers throughout the world who created the multiple hand-signage and logos which are reproduced in these pages. They influenced and inspired me to make this book.

Being in contact with this theme eventually inspired me to unify hand-signs into one single typeface which is used and represented in this handbook. This font was the subject of patient research, design and production for more than 10 years in my Swiss studio A N D where a few of our interns have been involved with it. Its final cut has been designed by Diana Stoen in the Summer 2002, retranscripted as a font by Moonkyung Choi and checked out by Sylvestre Lucia in 2005, and finally implemented by the font specialist Joachim Müller-Lancé. H-AND-S has been available online since March 2006.

My most sincere gratitude to my biological and visual family: Claudia D / Noa L / Monique J / Yvan D / Stephane L / Jean G / Pascale A / Michel C / Pablo C / Ethan C / Wolfgang W / Armin H / Thank you for the visual and moral input of: Rick R / Erik A / Patricia M / Markus H / Michael V / Joachim M-L / Mike K / Lee F / Aaron M / Jack S / Terry & Nori / Simone S / Fabienne M / Sarah W / Catherine W / Kara M / Manuel D / Daniel F / Bobby L / Tom & Michelle / Balz M / Lourdes L / Mary S / Chantal & Noemi / Anita G / David T / Allyson K / Lars M / Maurice B / Elke O / and you !

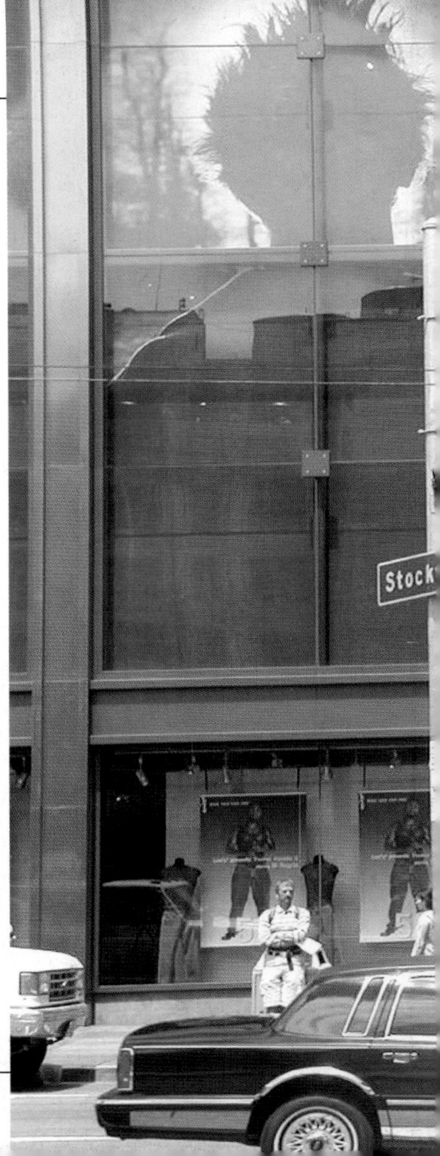

THIS BOOK IS DEDICATED
TO THE UNKNOWN
DESIGNER WHO DREW FOR
THE VERY FIRST TIME
THE THREE-STEP SEQUENCE
OF ONE HAND HOLDING
TWO CHOPSTICKS.

STYLIZATION

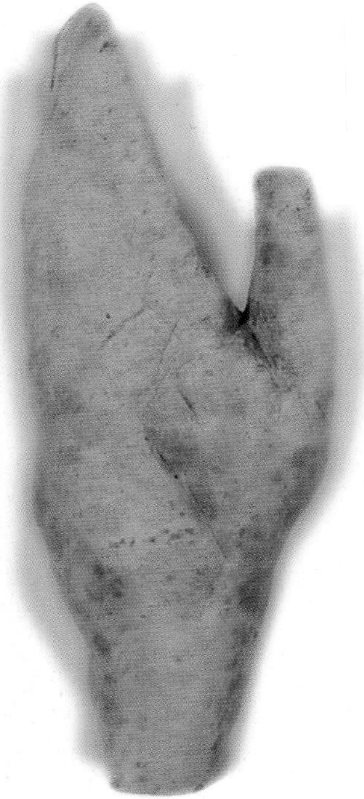

DECORATION

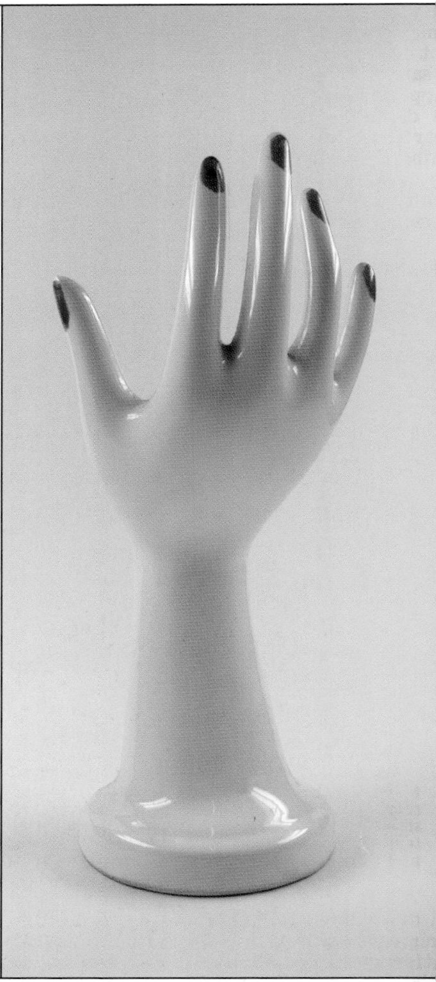

INFORMATION

REPRESENTATION

ı papier résistant,
·ment.
nt la forme d'une
sauf l'indicateur,
ıppeler l'attention
e desquelles on la
ɔurd'hui, que dans
ains dictionnaires,

re de divers coral-
onné les noms de

dissoudre par le g
procès retentissant.

Main chaude (L
réaliste, amusante e
riche de tons. (V. p

Main d'argent
Kader pour récomp
petite main d'argent
suivant la classe, se
le remplaça par une

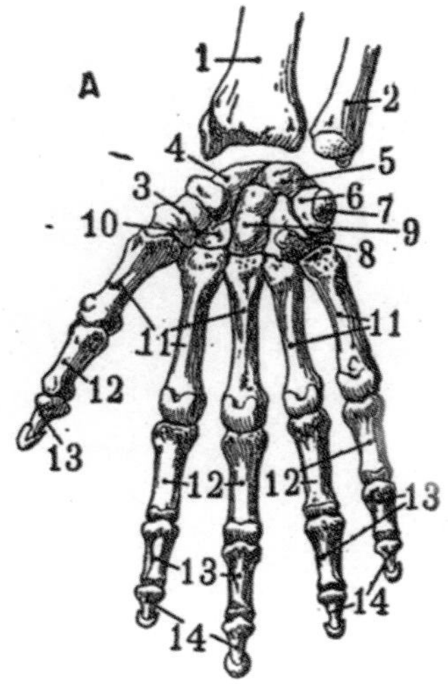

Main : A (1. Cubitus; 2. Radius; 3. T
6. Pyramidal; 7. Pisiforme; 8. Os crochu;
carpiens; 12. Phalanges; 13. Phalangènes;
superficiel des doigts; 2. Court abducteur du
teur du petit doigt; 5. Lombricaux.) — C
3. Paume; 4. Auriculaire; 5. Annulaire; 6.
nence thér

i donnent dans la
rêmement grande,
ition du pouce et

(Péloponnèse), dans
versants du Taygète
Laconie. Ses habita

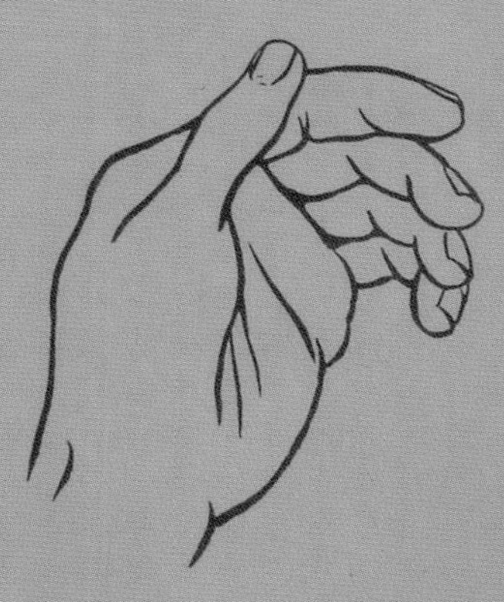

la main

In a dark small backstreet in a cheap Chinese restaurant in the middle of Manhattan's Chinatown, the hand-signage on the chopstick paper packaging on the table was exactly the same as the one I saw a long time ago, back in Europe as a little kid, experiencing Asian food for the first time.

There, far away from my home country I felt I was discovering the existence of a sort of unique sign language meant to be understood by all of us, everywhere on earth.

I have always wondered who was the very first person who ever drew the three hands on the paper of a chopstick package.

Was it the artistically inclined chef of the first exported Chinese restaurant? Was it the idea of a creative waitress? An ancient painter, ancestor of the graphic designer, who needed to pay for his meal with a drawing ? Or was it simply the invention of an imaginative customer in order to help others?

One fact is certain: the little sequence reproduced on the paper packaging, containing the couple of timeless chopsticks, explaining in three steps how to hold and handle them to eat, is now used all over the world. It has been redesigned many times in various sizes and colors and it is used on countless packaging for an infinite number of restaurants.

One could even say that this mini sequence has become today the perfect example of the representation of a global gesture.

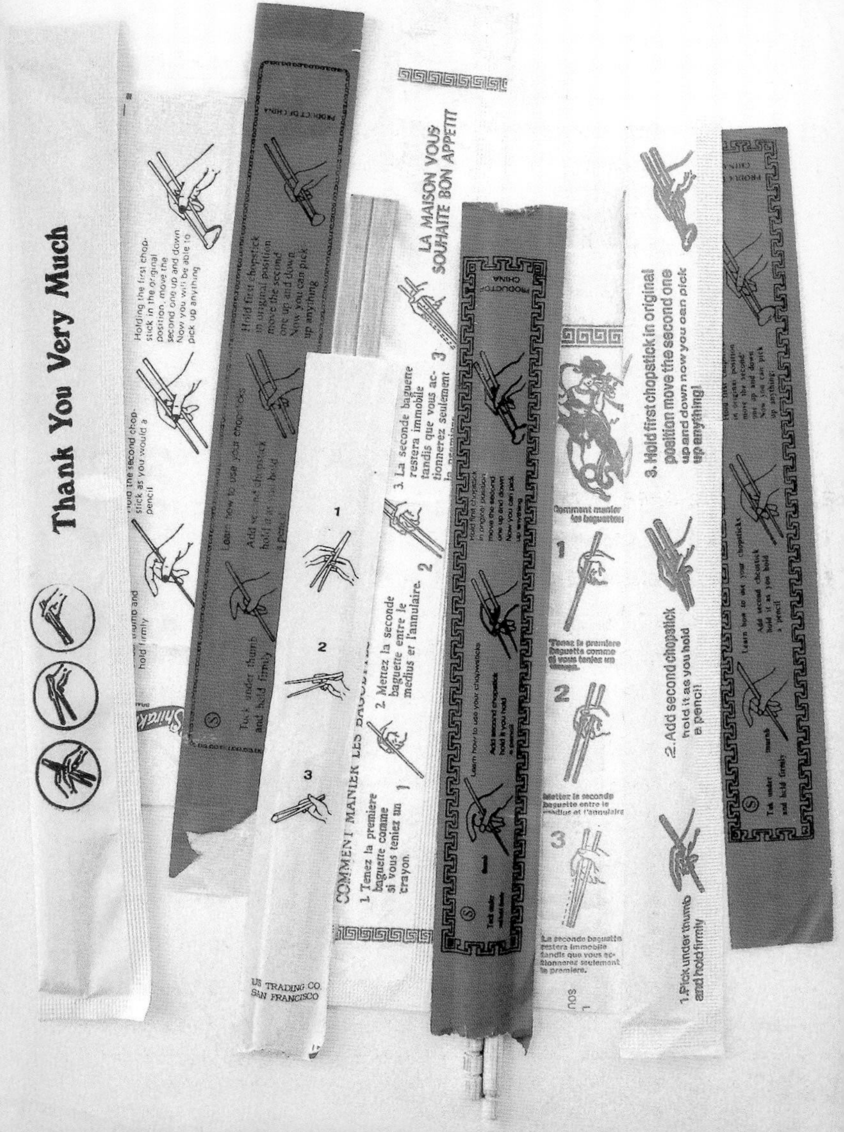

Thank You Very Much
Holding the first chopstick in the original position, move the second one up and down Now you will be able to pick up anything
Hold the second chopstick as you would a pencil
Tuck under thumb and hold firmly
PRODUCT OF CHINA
Hold first chopstick in original position move the second one up and down Now you can pick up anything
Learn how to use your chopsticks
Add second chopstick hold it as you hold a pencil
LA MAISON VOUS SOUHAITE BON APPETIT
COMMENT MANIER LES BAGUETTES
1 Tenez la premiere baguette comme si vous teniez un crayon.
2 Mettez la seconde baguette entre le medius et l'annulaire.
3 La seconde baguette restera immobile tandis que vous actionnerez seulement la premiere.
US TRADING CO. SAN FRANCISCO
Comment manier les baguettes
Tenez la premiere baguette comme si vous teniez un crayon.
Mettez la seconde baguette entre le medius et l'annulaire
La seconde baguette restera immobile tandis que vous actionnerez seulement la premiere.
1.Pick under thumb and hold firmly
2. Add second chopstick hold it as you hold a pencil
3. Hold first chopstick in original position move the second one up and down now you can pick up anything!

CONTENT

TO GIVE YOU A HAND

HAND – SIGN

MARK / TRACE / TAG / LABEL / IMPRINT
IDENTITY / BRAND / CHARACTER / INDICATION

HAND – SYMBOL

IDEAL / ENGAGEMENT / CONNECTION / ALLIANCE
EMBLEM / EXPRESSION / HELP / BLESSING / PRAYING

HAND – CODE

SIGNAL / FOCUS / WARNING / NOTICE
ORDER / GUIDE / DIRECTION / POSITION / INSTRUCTION

HAND – MOVEMENT

INSERTION / BRING / PLACE / DELIVERY
TRANSMISSION / PUSH / DRAG / TAKE / THROW

HAND – GESTURE

HANDLE / TWIST / GRASP / FIXATION
CLENCH / TRACTION / PULL / SWIPE / FRICTION

HAND – ICON

TOUCH / FEEL / WASH / MASSAGE / PRESS
CARESS / RUBBING / CARE / MANIPULATION

HAND – STYLE

ILLUSTRATION / PICTOGRAPH / LOGOGRAM / IDEOGRAPH /
TRANSLATION / ELEMENT / ALPHABET / WORD / SYSTEM

© Claudia Dallendörfer. San Francisco. Imprint from children in the fresh concrete of the sidewalk

Three million years ago,
in the long chain of creative evolution, the hominid
liberated his anterior limbs from the quadrupedal motion
progressively into a stable bipedal position.

He subsequently used his hands
improving the prehensile capabilities through the complete
opposition of the thumb toward the other digits.

Thus perfecting the sense of touch, and by gesturing,
used it as a means for expression and language.

He is able to externalize his thoughts
in unnumbered technical realizations which rise
with the formidable acceleration of the evolutive cultural
human process by completing in a decisive manner
the information transmitted to the other senses
– sight, hearing, smell and taste.

The empowered human registers new mental images,
which become more and more complex and consequently
develops his brain to interpret them.

Vis-a-vis with the pressure of vital requirements
he differentiates himself definitely
from other animal species through universal competition,
in particular by inventing fire.

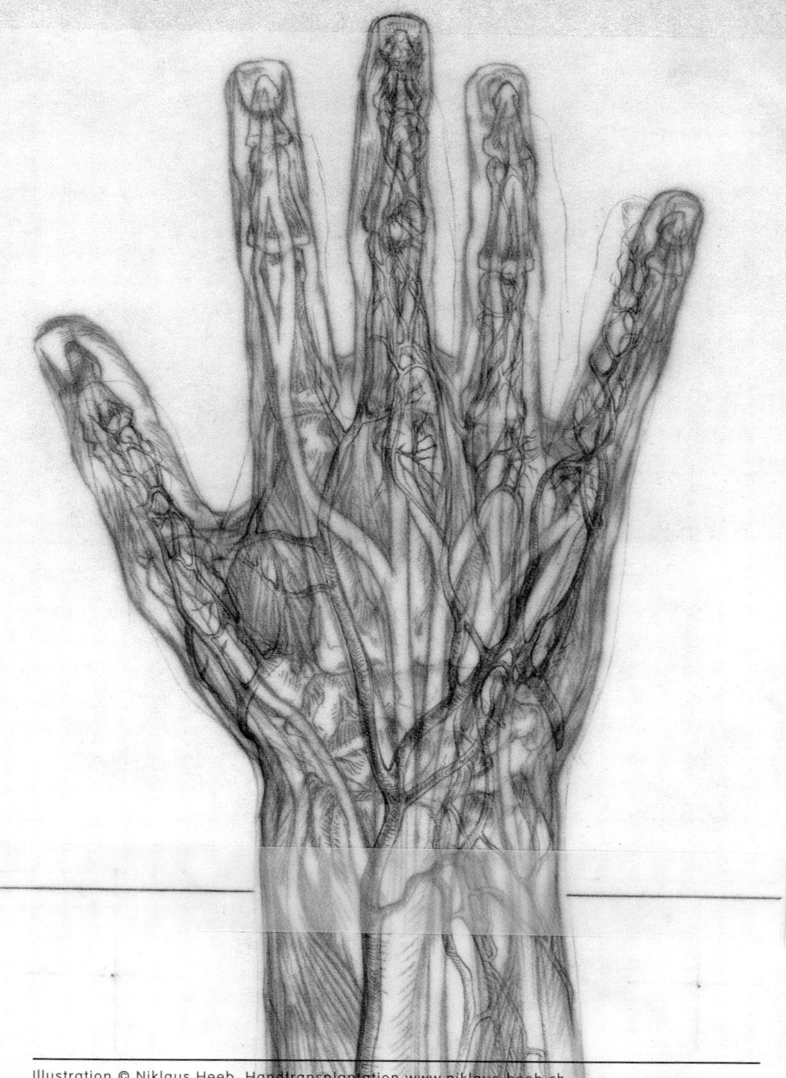

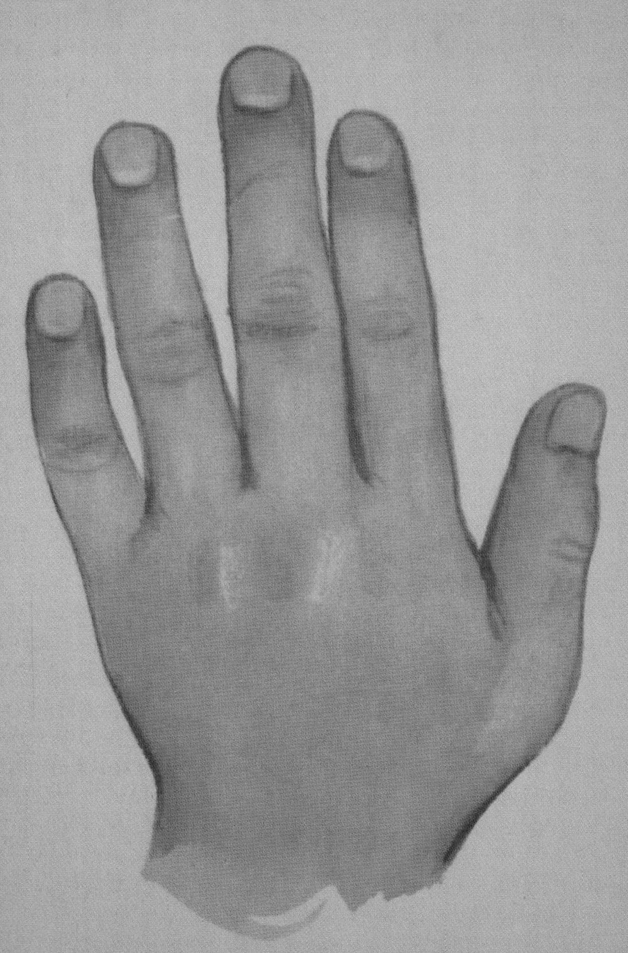

Français

Card found in San Francisco, at www.timelesstreasuressf.com

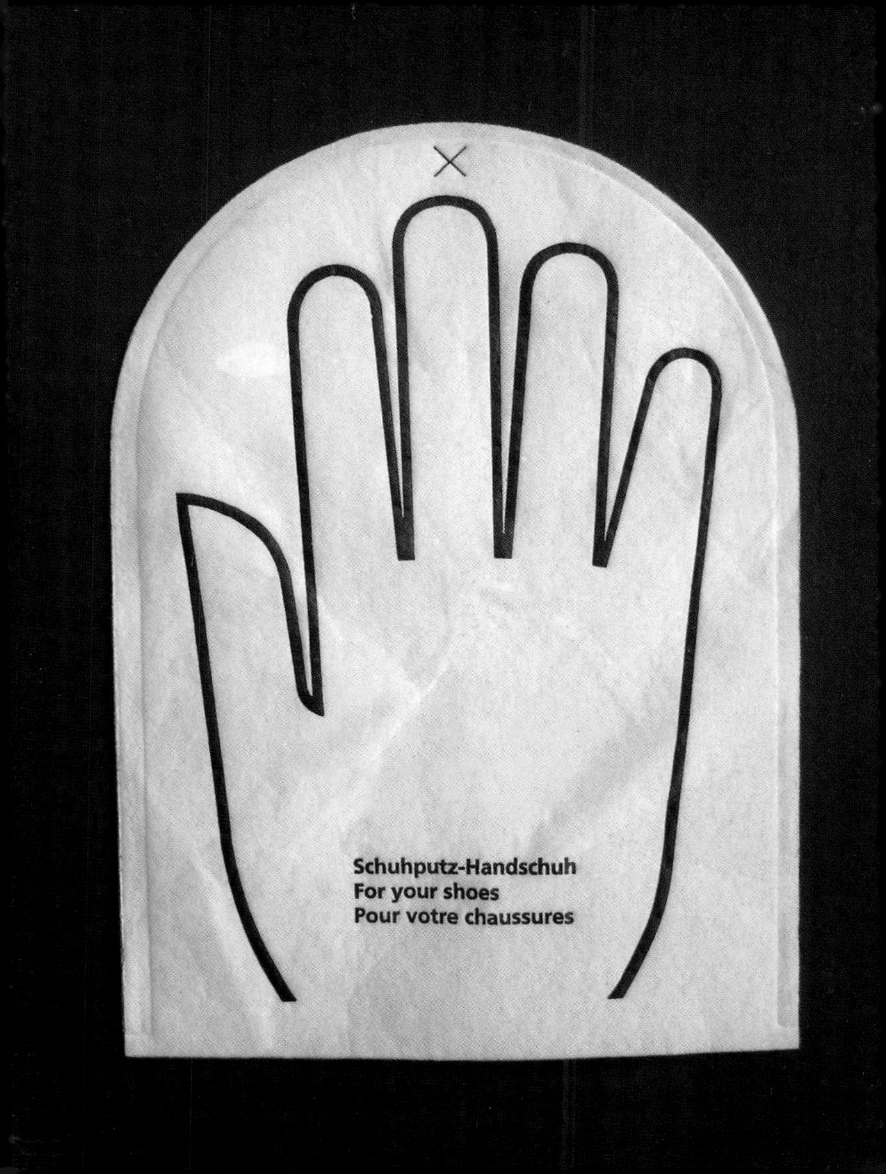

Schuhputz-Handschuh
For your shoes
Pour votre chaussures

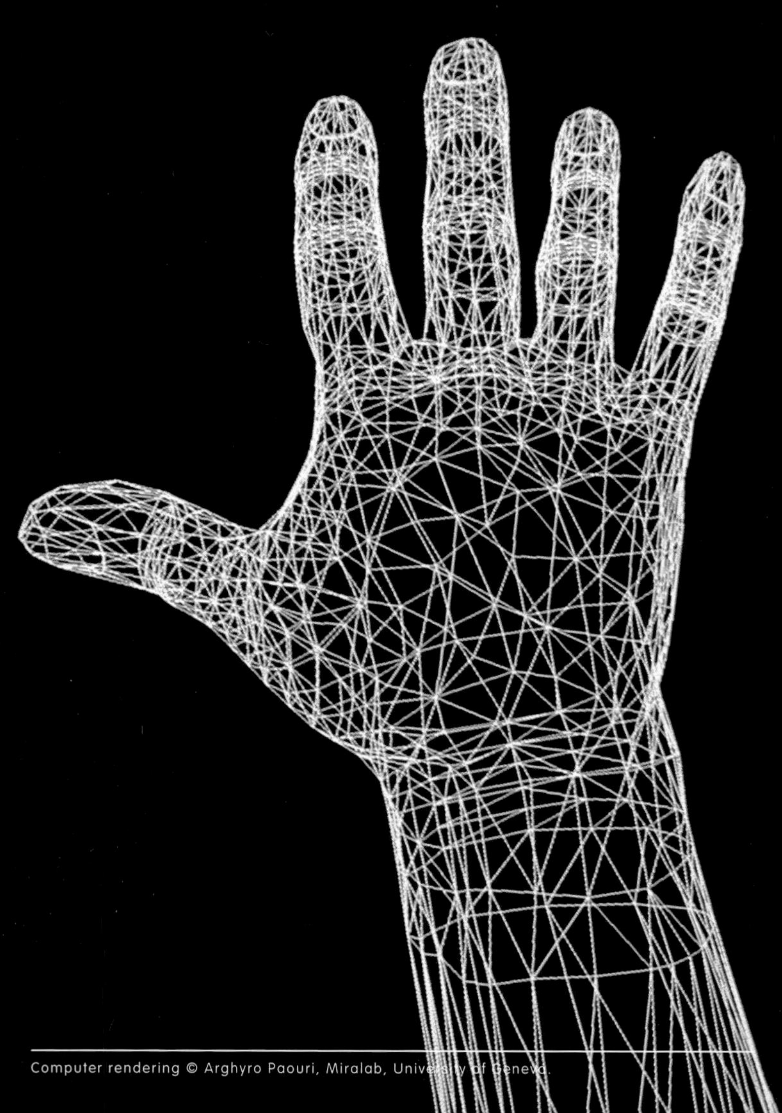

Through the combination of his prehensile and tactile capabilities the hand becomes the organ of knowledge by excellence, of the memorization of shapes and of the recognition of reality.

It is also the faithful servant of the surgeon. But it is also the vector of communication of human relations, of blessing or malediction, of caress or violence.

It is the hand which gives the human his personal print, helping him to solidify his thoughts by drawing, writing, artistic and musical expression and which are relevant to the culture and the prodigal life of the spirit.

At the dawn of humanity, only the hand was able to give new shape to matter. It is consequently a metaphor of the universe itself.

Both executrix and muse of human thought, the hand is the most beautiful prolongation of the brain. It is the hand that allowed the emergence of human kind, privileged heir of creation.

Therefore, the human being becomes creator himself, "by spirit and by hand", the human kind can take as an adage: "spiritu manuque".

PROF. CLAUDE VERDAN. **Surgeon. Founder of the Claude Verdan Foundation. Hand Museum, Lausanne, Switzerland. www.verdan.ch**

© Sridhar Rao / Kara Misenheimer. Hollywood, California. Celebrities leave their mark on the world – and on the pavement – in front of Graumann's Chinese Theater.

n Monroe
ondes
6-26-53

 10'000 year old rock art, Patagonia

HAND **SIGN**

MARK

TRACE

SIGNATURE

IMPRINT

IDENTITY

TO MARK

San Francisco, California

Berlin, Germany

San Francisco, California

Zurich, Switzerland

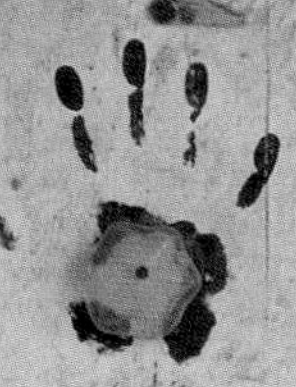

San Francisco, California

TO SIGNAL

San Francisco, California

Police car, Basel, Switzerland

BY HAND
HANDED BY
HANDED BY
MEMBER

Advertising, San Francisco, California

San Francisco, California

Basel, Switzeralnd

9977

itycarsh

Logo for a phone company, Rzezov, Poland

© Studio AND: Gloves store in the old town of Basel.

HANDSCHUHE

San Francisco, California

Basel, Switzerland

PALM READINGS
ENTRANCE
ENTRANCE
PALM & TAROT CARD READINGS by Christina TODAY
TAROT CARD READINGS
WALK-INS WELCOME
EMBARCADERO PSYCHIC
PALM & TAROT CARDS READING
PSYCHIC READING $10 SPECIAL
415-431-3868
PSYCHIC READINGS
By Christina
371-0077
127 Stevenson St
Permit #124193
Today $15.00

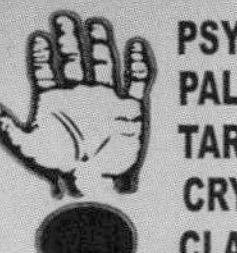
DISCOVER THE MYSTICAL
WORLD OF THE TAROT. ENTER
DOORS TO YOUR FUTURE WITH
HOLLY'S PSYCHIC READINGS
PSYCHIC
PALM
TAROT CARD
CRYSTAL
CLAIRVOYANT
READINGS
BY HOLLY

Monterey, California

Paris, France. © Daniel Furon. www.furon.net

San Francisco, California

OPEN

Psychic

PALM
READER

San Francisco, California

TO ADVERTISE

San Francisco, California

San Francisco, California

© Jean-Benoît Lévy. Pacifica, California. Palm reader for past, present and future.

MADAME ROSINKA
PAST·PRESENT
FUTURE TOLD
PALM READER

© Claudia Dallendörfer. Painted peace sign on the sidewalk

HAND	SYMBOL
EXPRESSION	
GREETING	
AFFIRMATION	
EMBLEM	
ALLEGORY	

TRIPLE
NOW! ON-AIR
HOWARD
STERN

→ openairs
stiller has

INTERNATIONAL BROTHERHOOD OF ELECTRICAL WORKERS
ORGANIZED NOV. 28, 1891
REG. U. S. PAT. OFF.

UNITE
AGAINST
UGLY

503

HIGH TIME
PEACE

CRUNCH
NO JUDGEMENTS

Park, San Francisco

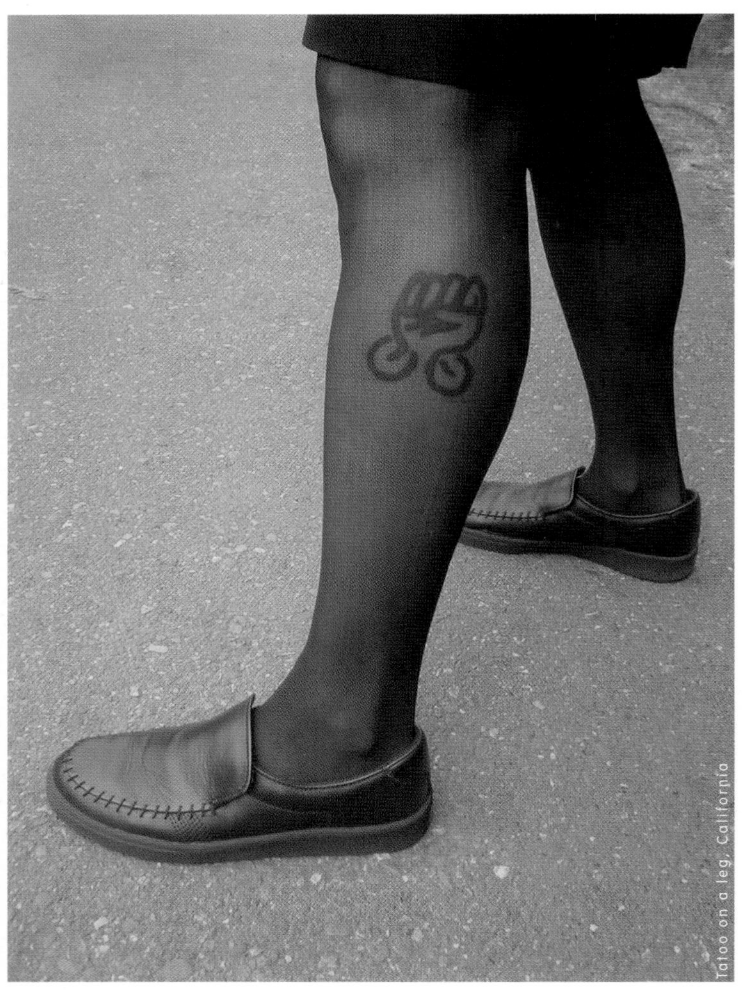

Tatoo on a leg, California

Stickers on a table of the "Coffee to the People", San Francisco

TO GREET

Basel, Switzerland

Corsier-sur-Vevey, Switzerland

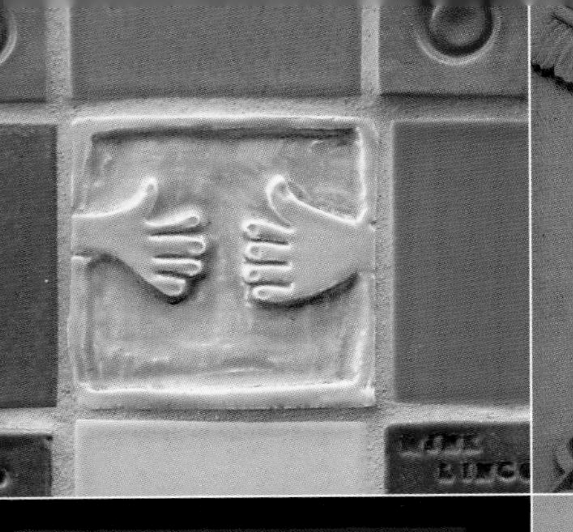

no enemy

LES AMIS

SAFETY BEGINS WITH
TEAMWORK

CENTRO PARA PERSONAS MAYORES
HORARIOS, HOURS:
LUNES A VIERNES
MONDAY TO FRIDAY
9:00 A.M. - 2:00 P.M.
BIENVENIDOS

WELCOME

San Francisco, California

Bus stop, San Francisco

Free posting wall, San Francisco

© Mariana Eliano / AP Photo. Madrid, 2004. People hold up their white painted hands to show a sign of peace a day after an estimated 200 people were killed from bombs placed

En 2004
comme en 1994,
Le racisme
enace
la démocratie
Appel gratuit
TOUCHE PAS À MON POTE
0800 55 4

STOP!
Install software BEFORE installing hardware!
technical help and assistance see the other side of this ca
NOT return this product to the store

pelastusrengas
amnesty international

© David Tartakover / Zoom 77. Freehand Design, 1987-2004. Mordechai Vanunu (who spent 18 years in prison for revealing Israel's nuclear secrets) presses the palm of his hand against the window of a police van, showing in "real time" to the media the date of his abduction by Mossad agents.

Hoppyland, Arizona

San Francisco, California

Demonstration, San Francisco, California

Peace demonstration, San Francisco

Der Tip Top Umzug
714 95 63
313 10 86

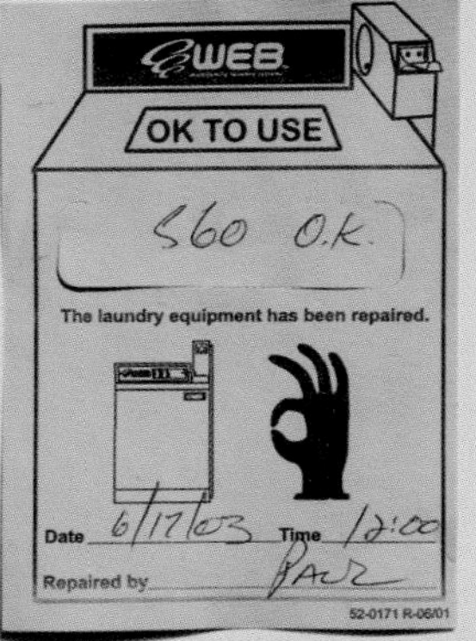
WEB
OK TO USE
560 O.K.
The laundry equipment has been repaired.
Date 6/17/03 Time 12:00
Repaired by
52-0171 R-06/01

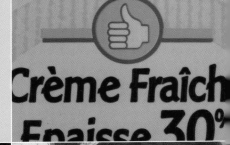

Crème Fraîch
Epaisse 30

THE WHITE STRIPES

LOOK
fuck you

San Francisco, California

Shirt found in San Francisco @ www.marthaegan.com

Bern, Switzerland

TO BLESS

San Francisco, California

Basel, Switzerland

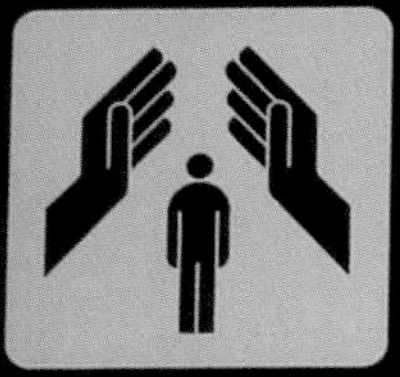

© Jean-Benoît Levy. Zurich airport. Before the departure

Chaplaincy ↑

Geschoss 2+3 (Galerie Sud TA)	
2-363	
2-366	Aeroflot
3-387	CGS Porter Service
2-372	Royal Jordanian
2-374	Malev Hungarian Airlines
2-381	A.T.R. AG ROYAL BRUNEI AIRLINES
2-392	
3-378	Flughafenpfarramt
3-384	
2-371	

UNHCR
United Nations High Commissioner for Refugees

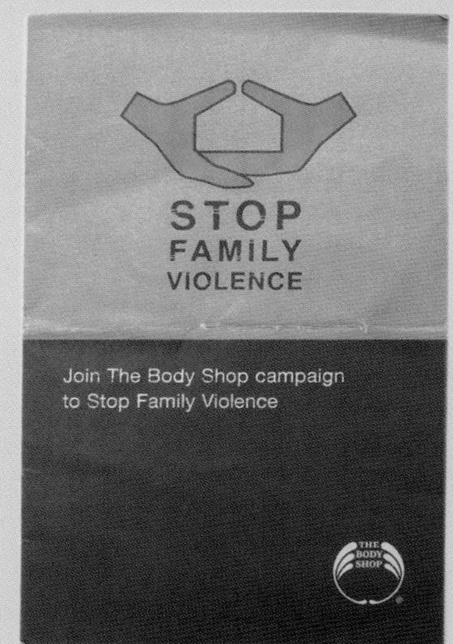
STOP
FAMILY
VIOLENCE
Join The Body Shop campaign
to Stop Family Violence
THE BODY SHOP

SafePlace SM

Safe Surrender Site
Zona Protegida de Renuncia a su Hijo (a)
交付新生嬰兒的安全地點

THE SEMIOTICS OF HANDS IN COMMUNICATION

AARON MARCUS

To discuss the meaning of hand signs, one must clarify terminology and dimensions of semiotics in understanding the attributes and functions of hand signs in human communication.

As the analyst Abraham Moles described it in his book about information theory and aesthetic perception (Moles, 1971), communication can be for one or more of these objectives: to provide information, persuasion or aesthetics.

Informational communication can be translated from one medium to another. For example, one can transform a table of numbers into a chart, or a prose text into an informative illustration. One can even test to see if the content has been conveyed accurately and precisely.

Likewise, much of persuasive communication can be transformed and translated from one medium to another; however, aesthetic communication cannot. Each medium has unique attributes, although one can make analogies, like transforming a painting to music, or a poem to a drawing.

No matter where hands appear, in three-dimensional signage, in printed publications, or in computer-based media with human-computer interfaces, people send and receive content of all three kinds. To understand the "meaning" of these signs, we need to consider semiotics, which studies the attributes and use of signs.

The four dimensions of semiotics according to the theory of Peirce (Buchler, 1955) are the lexical, syntactic, semantic, and pragmatic dimensions.

Lexical issues concern how one produces signs, that is, the physical processes involved. Are the images of hands painted, or printed? Unique images or mass reproductions? Digital or analogue medium? Here, one can begin to classify and describe different hand signs by the techniques of their production.

Syntactic issues concern the perceptual aspects of signs. Are the images black-and-white or multi-colored? Linear images or photographic images? Gigantic or minuscule? Static or dynamic? Here, one can begin to classify and describe different hand signs by their visual, tactile, even acoustic characteristics.

Semantic issues concern how one sign stands for another. What does the image of the hand denote? Connote? How is it linked to one or more references? Here, one can begin to classify and describe different hand signs by their referential character. To what does the pointing hand point? From?

In this realm of semantics, consideration of the many techniques of rhetoric arises. For example, the technique of metaphor refers to substitution of one thing for another.

General store, California

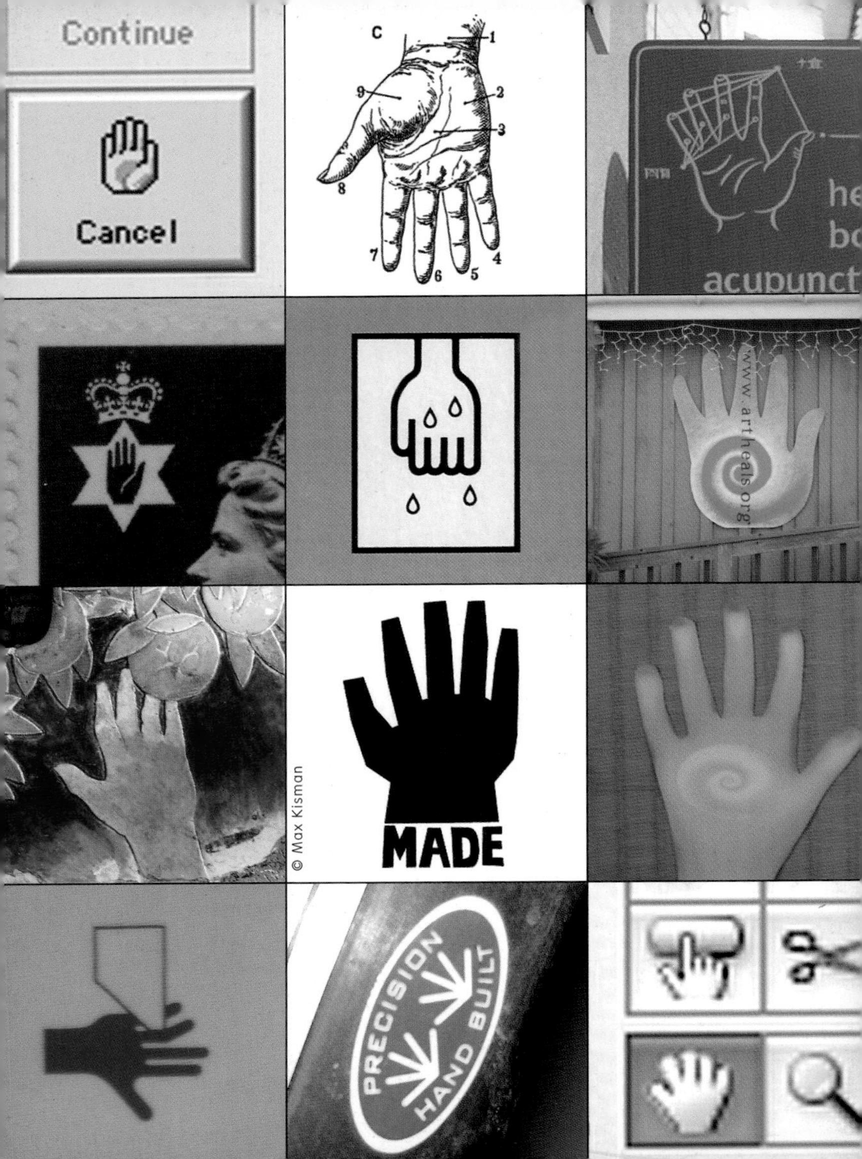
Continue
Cancel
www.artheals.org
© Max Kisman
MADE
PRECISION
HAND BUILT

Peet's Coffee San Francisco

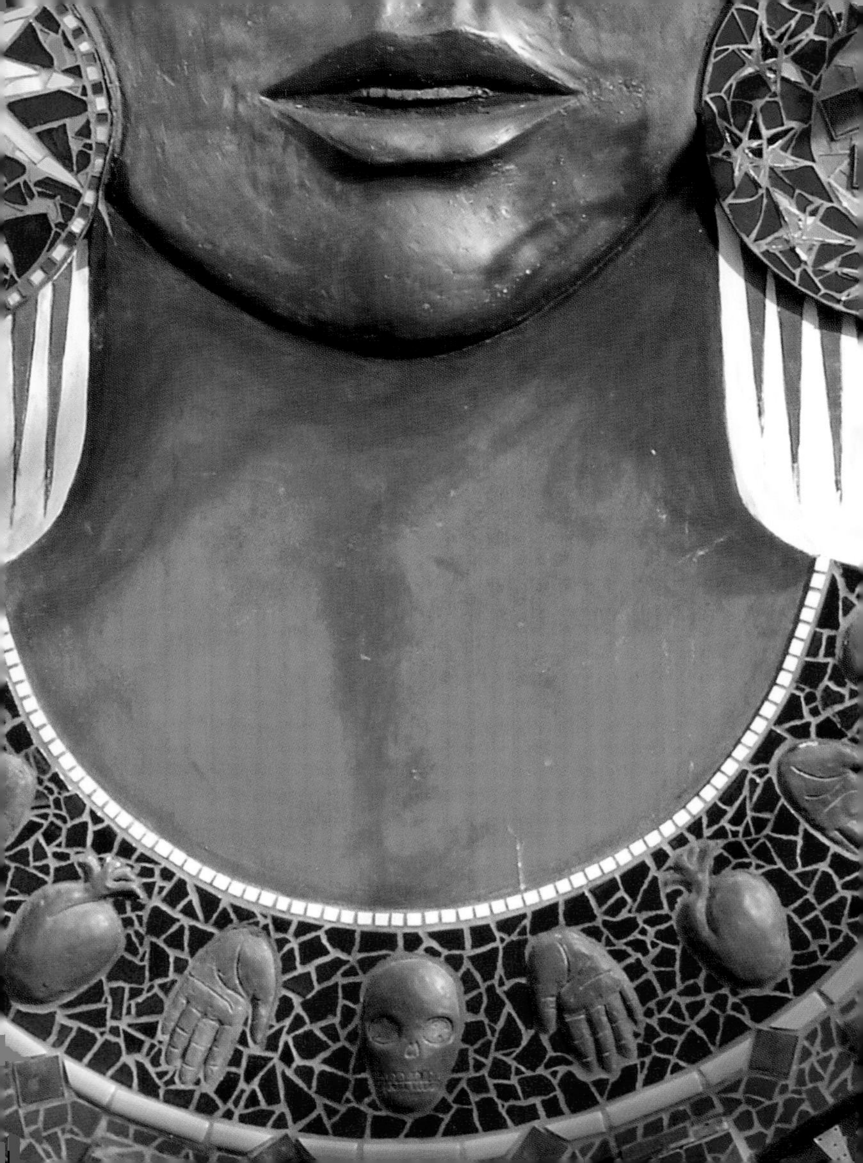

Pragmatic issues concern how the signs are consumed, used, or read. Are they familiar or obscure? Legible and/or readable, or not? Memorable or easily forgotten? Confusing or unambiguous? Here, one can begin to classify and describe different hand signs by their use, function, absorption, and/or appeal.

Hand signs can be icons, symbols, or indices according to semiotics.

Icons look like that which they represent and are seemingly self-revealing. Symbols, like the phonograms, or sound-signs, of our writing systems, are abstract and must be learned. Indices, like a muddy hand print on a wall, are a memento of its maker, linked by cause and effect, time and space, to that which formed them.

Hand signs can be photographic or photo-realistic (very immediate and self-explanatory), pictograms and pictographic (like the markings of prehistoric peoples), or ideograms (images of concepts related to how signs function in pointing, marking, tracing or indicating).

Hands can be individual, unique signs, or part of a system, like those in ancient Egyptian hieroglyphics, modern traffic signs, or at international sports events. Different times, different peoples, different technologies have produced hand signs.

Hand signs are fundamental to human experience. They are an essential part of the history of graphical story telling since the earliest peoples traced outlines of their own hands on cave walls with charcoal. The hand itself, in its life lines, in its tattoos and scars, bears witness to a long past, a vital present, and an enduring future.

REFERENCES:

Philosophical Writings of Peirce / **Buchler, Justus, ed. / Dover Publications, New York / 1955 ISBN 0-486-20217-8 / Chapter 7 of this book summarizes Peirce's theory of semiotics.**

A Theory of Signs / **Eco, Umberto / 1976 / University of Indiana Press / Bloomington, IN.**

Metaphors in User-Interface Design / **Marcus, Aaron / 1998 / ACM SIGDOC (Special Interest Group on Documentation) / Vol, 22, No.2, May 1998, pp. 43-57, ISSN 0731-1001**

Principles of Effective Visual Communication for Graphical User Interface Design / **Marcus, Aaron / 1995 / in Readings in Human-Computer Interaction, 2nd Edition / Ed. Baecker, Grudin, Buxton, & Greenberg, Morgan Kaufman, Palo Alto / pp. 425-441 / ISBN: 1-55860-246-1**

Graphical User Interfaces / **Marcus, Aaron / 1997 / Chapter 19, in Helander, M.G., Landauer, T.K., and Prabhu, P., Eds. / Handbook of Human-Computer Interaction / Elsevier Science, B.V., The Hague, Netherlands / pp. 423-44 / ISBN 0-444-4828-626**

Icon and Symbol Design Issues for Graphical User Interfaces / **Marcus, Aaron / 1996 Chapter 13 in del Galdo, Elisa M., and Jakob Nielsen, eds. / pp. 257-270 International User Interfaces / Wiley, New York / ISBN 0-471-12965**

Graphic Design for Electronic Documents and User Interfaces / **Marcus, Aaron / 1992 Addison-Wesley, Reading MA / ISBN: 0-201-54364-8 (also available in Japanese)**

An Introduction to the Visual Syntax of Concrete Poetry / **Marcus, Aaron / 1974 Visible Language / Vol. 8, No. 4 / pp. 333-360 / Autumn 1974**

Visual Rhetoric in a Pictographic-Ideographic Narrative / **Marcus, Aaron / 1979 In Proceedings of the Second Congress of the International Association for Semiotic Studies pp. 1501-1508 / Mouton Publishers, New York**

Symbolic Constructions / **Marcus, Aaron / 1973 / Typographische Monatsblaetter / Vol. 92, No. 10 / pp. 671-683 / St. Gallen, Switzerland**

Information Theory and Aesthetic Perception / **Moles, Abraham / 1971 University of Illinois Press / Chicago**

AARON MARCUS. **President of Aaron Marcus and Associates, Inc.. Visual communications analyst & designer. Lives + works in Berkeley, California, USA, www.AMandA.com.**

San Francisco, California

© Jean-Benoît Lévy / Cal train station. San Jose, California

WALK
YOUR
BIKE
Caltra

© Studio AND / Flag on Broadway / On the way to Jack Stauffacher, San Francisco

HAND CODE

SIGNAL

WARNING

COMMAND

GUIDE

DIRECTION

© Chih Fan Ting. Model: Daniel Binuya

Prilly, Switzerland

Private

Outlook Express

An error occurred while printing.
The printer can not be found.
OK

CODE
BLAUPUNKT

Private residence, California

Santa Cruz, California

Traffic light, San Francisco, California

© Studio AND / Basel, Switzerland. Shoe store in Basel.

BAZAR
SCHUH

ORDER
BURRITO

50 % Fruchtanteil/de
pasteurisiert/
Tipp siehe
Voir conseil au
Vedi consiglio sul

OTTO'S

ACHTUNG
ATTENTION
ATTENZIONE
!
PTT

PTT 236.27-1 (114123) 2.91 4,5 Mio. PB

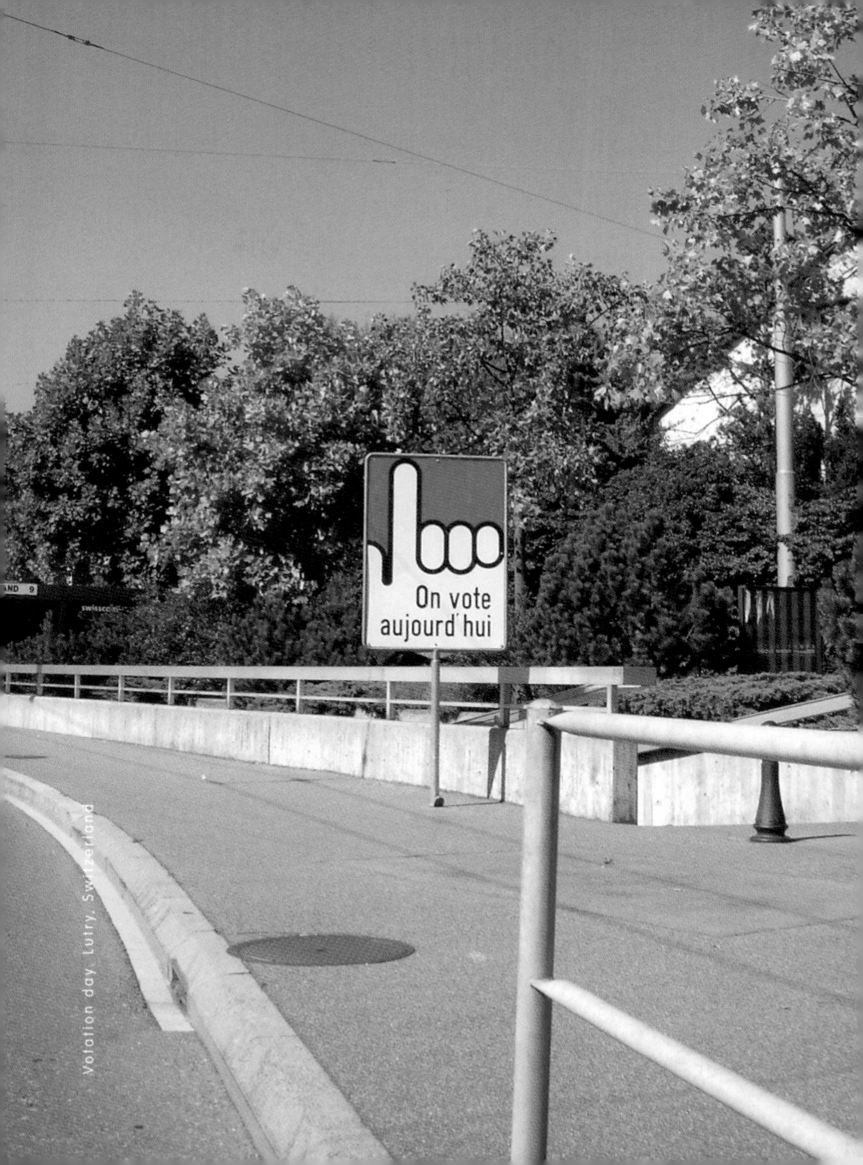
On vote
aujourd'hui

Votation day, Lutry, Switzerland

limm zwe
Dieses
Wochenende
Abstimmung
TZT
O SIE
LOTTO TOTO 31
TOTO-X
TOTO-R
jedesmal
chaque fois
ogni volta

Border with France, Basel, Switzerland

© Studio AND. Pick – Order – Pay. Bagel shop in San Francisco.

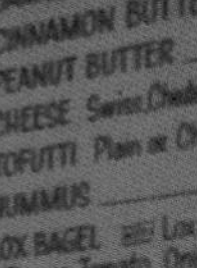
PICK UP
HERE
JAM or HONEY or
CINNAMON BUTTE
PEANUT BUTTER
CHEESE
TOFUTTI
HUMMUS
LOX BAGEL
16th Street
odwalla

TO GUIDE

Montreux, Switzerland

Paris, France

INSTANT
PASSPORT & ID PHOTO
20 MIN. FILM
PROCESSING
PASSPORT PHOTO
FINGERPRINTING
PAL–SECAM–NTSC
VIDEO CONVERSION
B & W APS SLIDES
FAX SERVICE

San Francisco, California

© Claudia Dallendörfer / Store in Saint Louis, France

PRIX EN BAISSE
PRIX EN BAISSE
PRIX EN BAISSE
PRIX EN BAISSE

open
coffee
Hot Food
to Go

当店の
おすすめ品

2ND FL.

TO
BEACH

San Francisco, California

TO POINT OUT

Poster, San Francisco, California

San Francisco, California

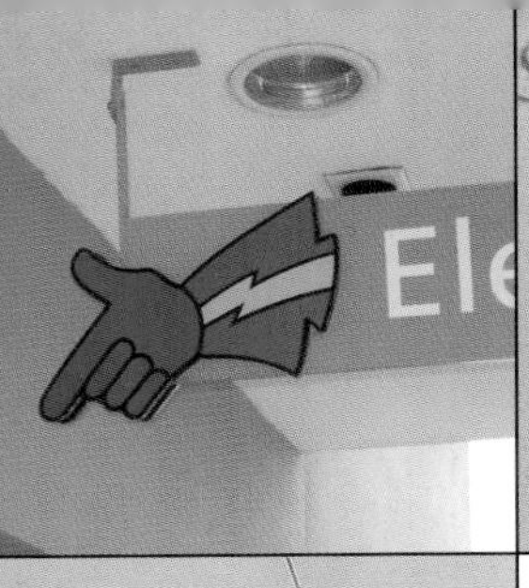
Ele

Sample - Not for
1401141

EXTER

RETURNED
TO
SENDER
NOT DELIVERABLE AS
UNABLE TO FORWARD
DO NOT USE THIS WRAPPER AGAIN
NEW YORK, NY 10017

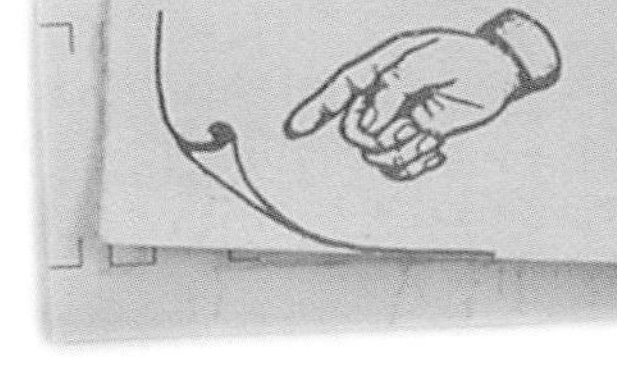
Hier aufreissen

RESTROOMS

Baslerstab

•COPIES
•TRANSLATIONS
•FAX

HANIX
diva♥diva
Apparel Accessorie

Please ring bell

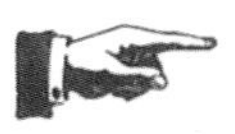

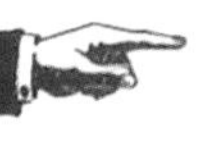

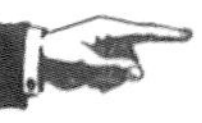

San Francisco, California

© Studio AND. Push button for traffic light, Basel, Switzerland.

METROPOLIS, HANDS AND INTERFACES

ERIK ADIGARD

In Fritz Lang's 1926 movie Metropolis, Freder, the main character asks, "It was their hands that built this city of ours, father. But where do the hands belong in your scheme?" His father answers, "In their proper place – the depths."

Today, we still live among countless disembodied servants, assistants and workers that we only see as "interfaces". We walk by them, drive in them, play with them and communicate through them. We hold them, control them and talk to them. Or is it them talking to us?

Mechanical language is conceived by humans. Machines, physical or digital and languages, spoken or codified, are the defining factors of modernity. This language comes in the form of words, signs and pictograms that turn into a stream of commands forever adaptive in the context they are meant to serve.

Language is intrinsic to the survival of all systems and as such it has an autonomic momentum that may already exist beyond our grasp.

Machines, like humans, are meant to touch and to be touched, so they come with hands, a reassuring reflection of ourselves in an attempt to convince us of their existence as avatars of the workers they have replaced.

Hands are attached to bodies; therefore they also reaffirm the presence of the machinery they belong to.

Intella-Pay
Intella-Pay

NO CHANGE GIVEN
Insert Card As Shown
Stripe Down

1 2 3
4 5 6
7 8 9
CANCEL 0 ENTER
PRESS TO BEGIN

Insert Bill(s) Face Up
1 START
2 PAY

3 TICKET
WARNING: MONITORED SECURITY ALARM - MACHINE EMPTIED DAILY

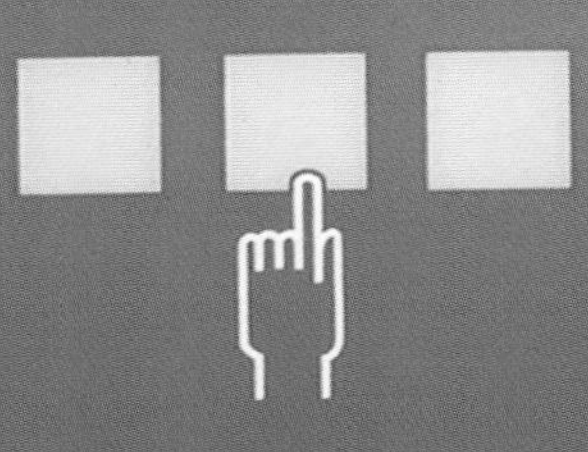
INSTRUCTIONS
Select
Grade
Above

APPUYEZ POUR

MINUTES
Within the U.S./International flat rates vary.

SOLD OUT
WHEN
LIT
PUSH
TO SELECT
Machine # 9

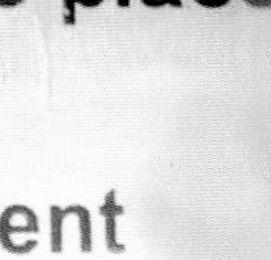
e place

gent

Fr
on vert

z-le
e-brise

TICKET

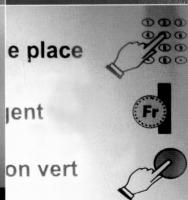

ON HEADLESS PROXY

Graphical interface is on everything: remote controls, computer screens, ovens, cars, airplanes and buildings. And it is everywhere on our physical sphere and our infosphere.

Like machines and devices, interfaces are pervasive. They clone each other, always appearing in the same shapes and forms.

Interfaces seem to always be on: they hum, click, vibrate, ring and crunch, and when they seem passive, they are still engaged. Whether on or off, they continue to convey in their own machine language. In their own silent way, for better or for worse, interfaces tirelessly tell us how to use them.

This language, like the machines, is intrinsic to countless functions that we run through each day. Like the machinery that it speaks for, it is industrial by nature. It uses the same forms of stillness and shapes of coolness.

No matter what our interpretation may be, these machines and devices do express their humanity through language and in doing so, they make the impossible claim to become social entities.

These billions of iconic hands are ambiguously alive like a population busy doing their best to guide and show and tell by pushing, pulling, pressing, lifting and swapping.

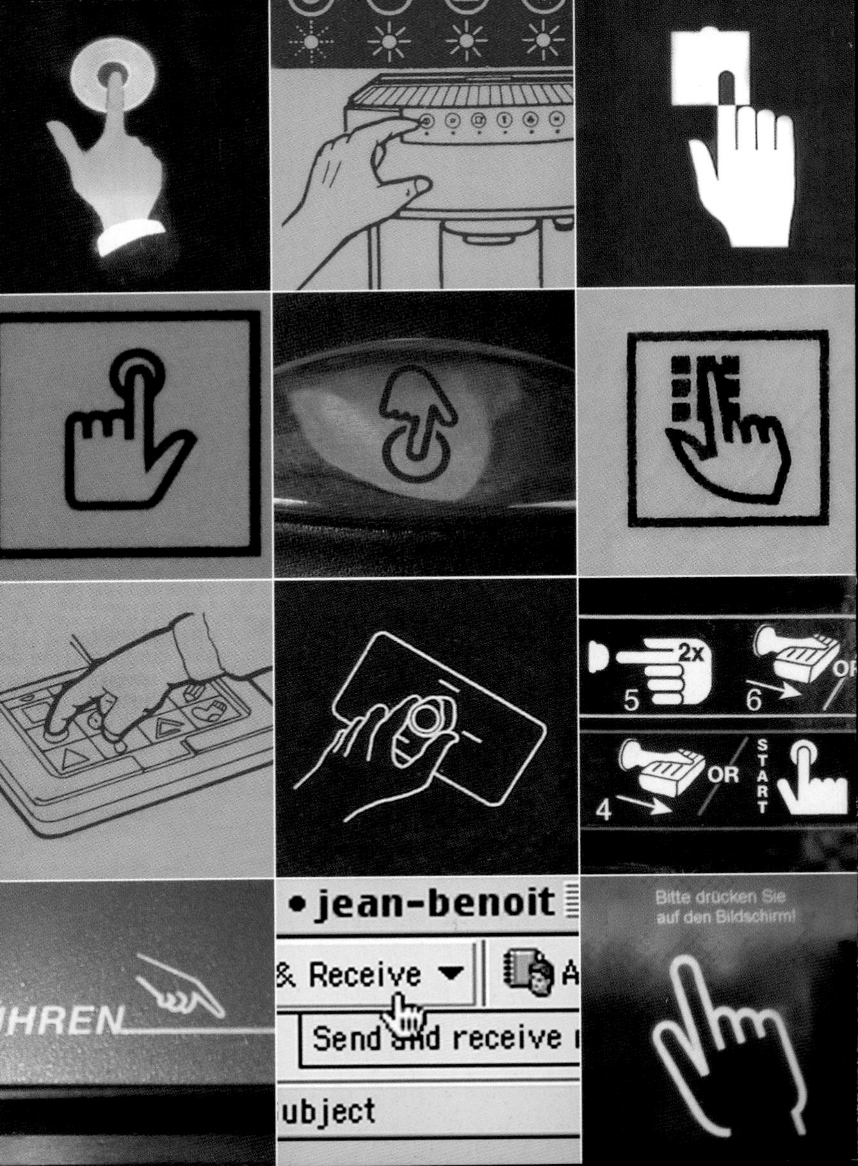

2x
5
6
OR
4
OR
START

HREN
• jean-benoit
& Receive
Send and receive
ubject

Bitte drücken Sie
auf den Bildschirm!

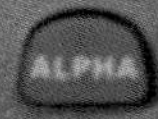

San Francisco, California

ON SPEECHLESS TALK

Pictograms, by design, do not attract attention, yet they are highly visible, clear and decisive. They are shorthand narrative, but it would be wrong to mistake it for a primitive language. Good pictorial instructions have to rely on sophisticated syntax in part because people can easily be confused by diagrammatic communications but mostly because such language is intended for an international reach. It is the one global language we all share, a reminder that it was primarily inspired 50 years ago by the rise of transportation and international travel. Today, technology, economy, culture and language are all pulling us into the challenges of globalism.

Standardization comes at a cost. We often resent machines that make us translate what at first glance will look like hieroglyphs. In the first second, we curse, we scratch our heads and we look around to check that no one can witness our state of confusion. We soon recognize human forms that reassure us of the machine's good intentions.

Good pictograms are economical shapes with minimal but perfect detailing. They reflect the essence of the devices on which they exist: square or rounded steel and plastic.

They are required to exist on background of eggshell, matte, or other non-glare finish.

swisscom
117
118
144
175
111
1151
1152
1153
1154
1159
143
162
164
dit cards
ecific credit card surcharges
card
PIN/NIP

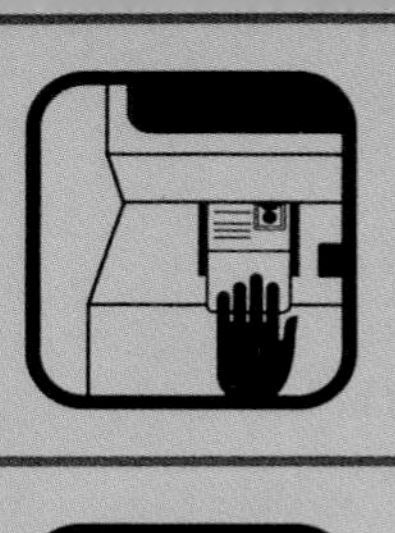

US-VISIT

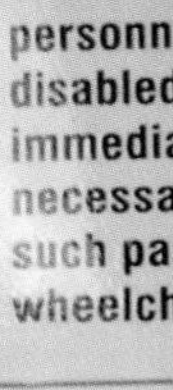
In an emer
evacuation
personnel
disabled pa
immediate
necessary,
such passe
wheelchai

To stop tra
emergenc
emergenc
located ne
destinatio
each end

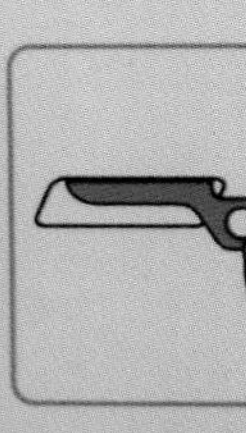
If instruct
doors in e
handle do
door side

To talk to
press inte
release b
operator
then spea

Pictograms are momentous signs: given their contexts, they can have drifting connotations. A shape not only tells us how to operate a machine, but it stands ready for additional interpretations – mobility, corporate absolutism, urban myths, design culture or simply a sense of complicity, as if a friendly agent was literally standing guard next to us. And because hands are sexless we can unconsciously attach them to our preferred gender.

Iconic representations have never tried to be realistic instead they attempt to transcend the physicality of their subject. Pictograms, like the machines they live on, have no personality, no desires, no opinions and no emotions. They are odorless, voiceless and colorless. They blend into millions of other pictograms that we pass by each day.

ON HANDLESS MANUALS

As we increasingly hear about artificial intelligence, posthumanism and transhumanism, efficiency seeks the elimination of all friction: will hands disappear?

Beyond their role as semantic devices, hand pictograms are an opportune commentary that, for so many centuries, our hands have been used to complete mechanical and repetitive gestures, the same gestures that have been taken over by machines.

The few gestures that remained in the control of humans were to "handle" the pumping of gas, the counting of bank notes and the punching of metro tickets. It is these last activities that pictograms are representing.

The first tool was a hand and the last tool deserves to be a hand, but what happens when tools escape our grip to become mere buttons? We still need to grasp and hold objects in order to make contact with the physical world, so we intently hold our computer mouse to touch information, we obsessively hold our cell phone to talk and now we choose our iPod as dancing companion. These devices are holding our hands and, if anything it is our eyes doing the touching.

Increasingly, machines will become more intimate with us, to, one day, become a part of us. Then, as we pass through the machines around us, it will be the ones within us that will be doing the talking, the demands, the negotiations, the background checks and the handling! Until this "humachine" day, we will continue our casual and innocent encounters with the world of signs and pictograms.

If we can invent and master the right language, we can conceive that the day all functions are taken over by machines, we will inherit our hands as the ultimate tool, the one of inter-human communication.

ERIK ADIGARD. **Graphic designer specialized in branding & graphic design systems. Lives and works in Sausalito, California. www.madxs.com**

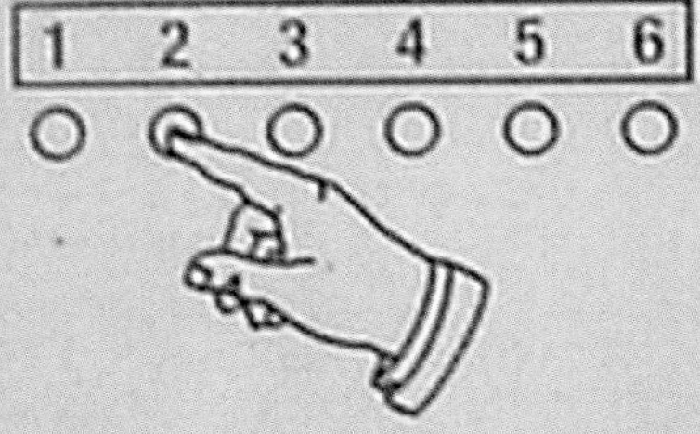

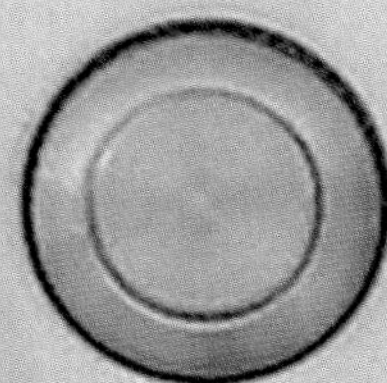

© Claudia Dallendörfer. Parking at the Zurich airport

CASH-Karte
CASH-Karte
einschieben!
3.
STOP
INFO
4.
Meldung
"Karte entnehmen"
abwarten!

1

Fachtüre öffnen
Gepäck einstellen

ouvrez le casier
placez vos bagages

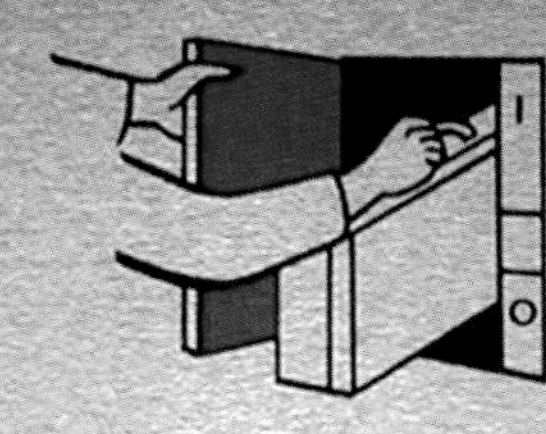

2

Betrag einwerfen

introduisez la
monnaie

3

Türe verschliessen
Schlüssel abziehen
und gut aufbewahren

fermez la porte à clef
retirez et conservez
soigneusement la clef

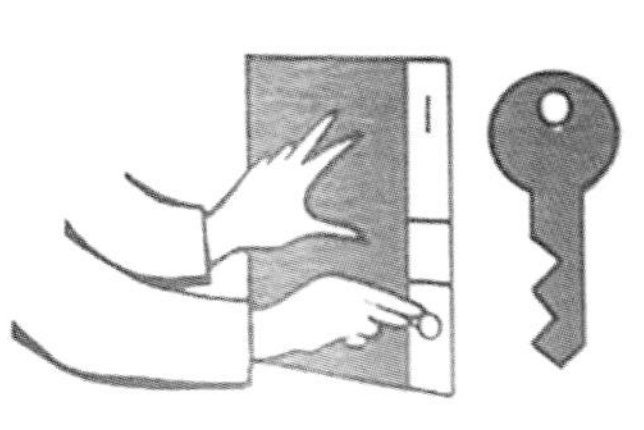

© Claudia Dallendörfer. Instructions of the luggage box in the Swiss train stations

HAND MOVEMENT

INSERT

SWIPE

TEAR

PULL

THROW

TO INSERT

AVANT
D'INSÉRER VOS
PIECES
N'OUBLIEZ PAS
DE VALIDER LE
NOMBRE DE
BILLETS.
ENFIN INSEREZ
VOS PIECES

Payement instruction Switzerland

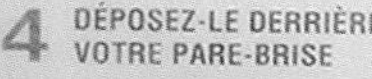

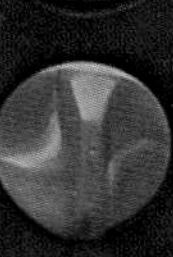

Vevey, Switzerland

1 STOP
2 LISTEN FOR TONE
3 DEPOSIT COINS

5 - 10 - 25
U.S. COINS ONLY

San Francisco, California

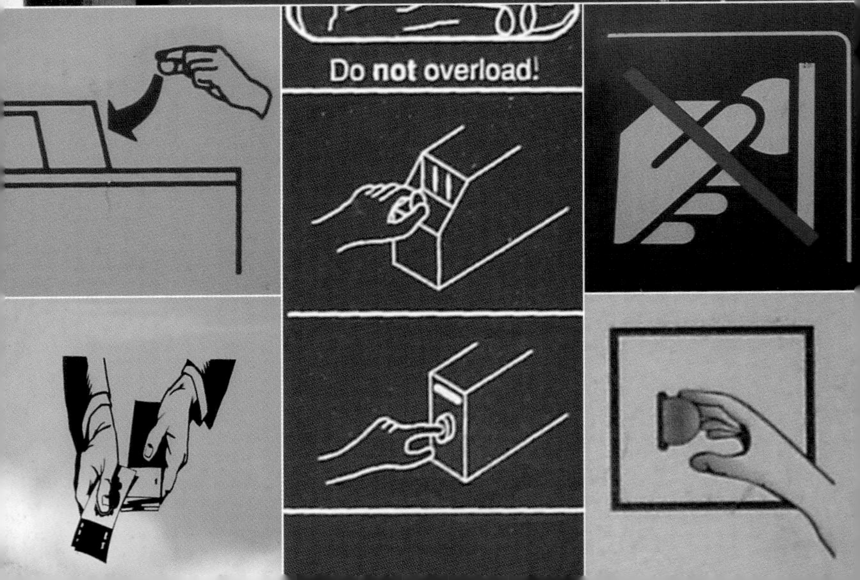

Do **not** overload!

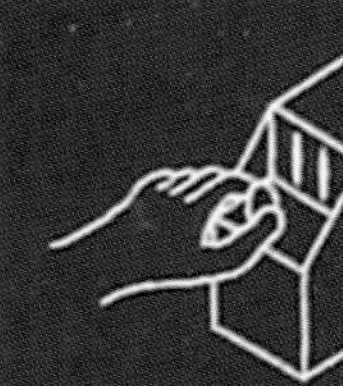

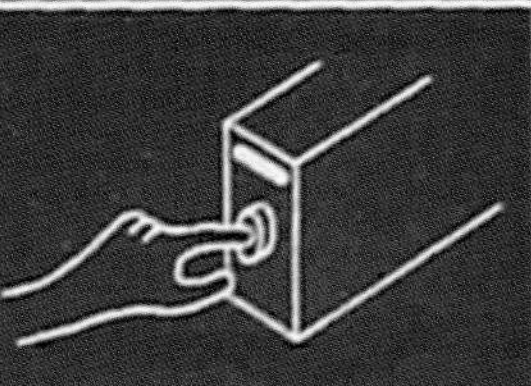

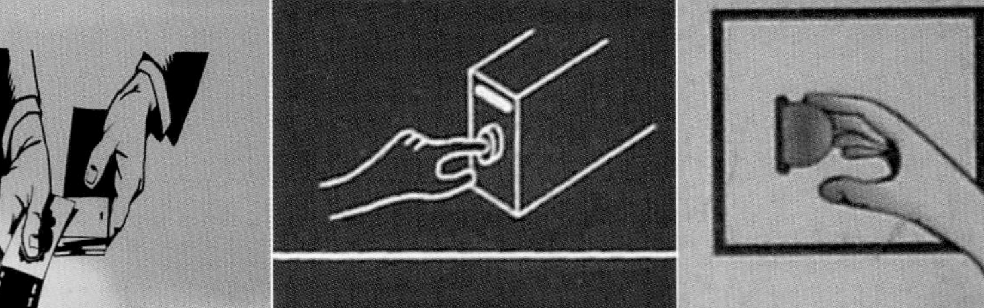

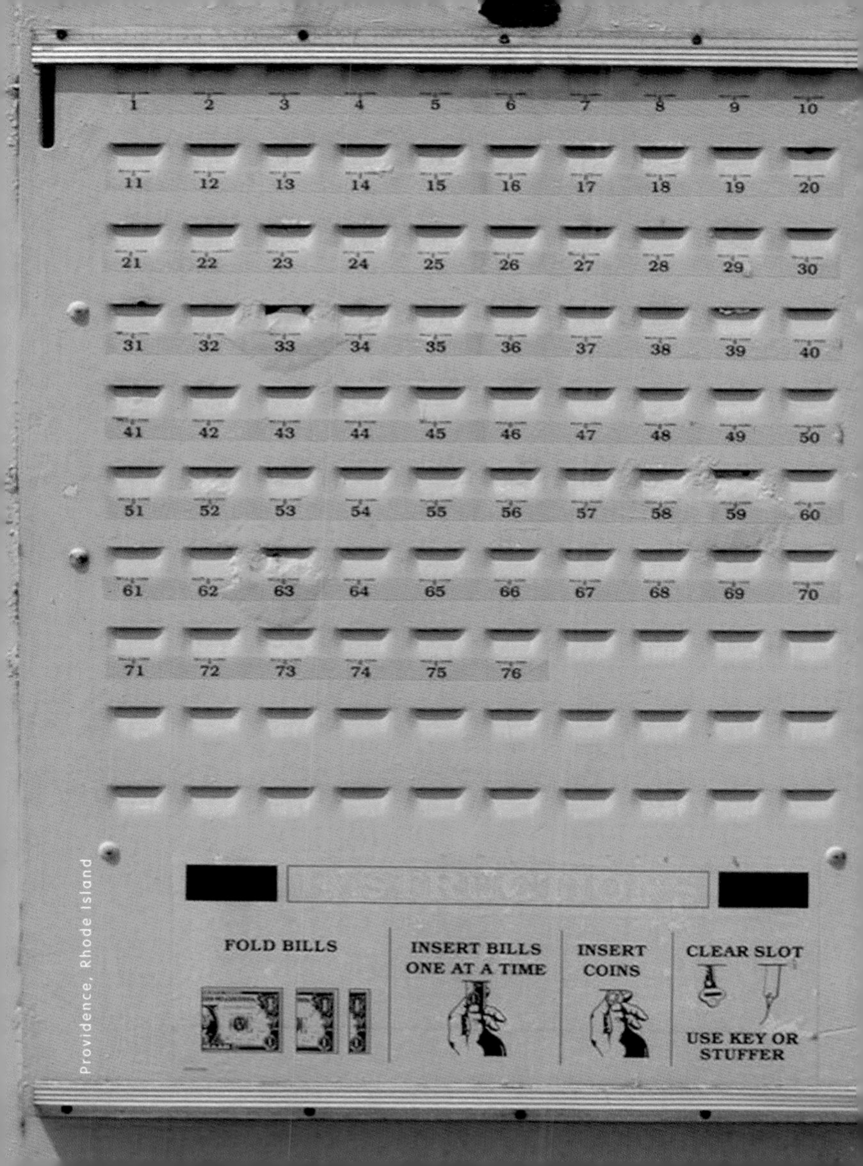

1 2 3 4 5 6 7 8 9 10
11 12 13 14 15 16 17 18 19 20
21 22 23 24 25 26 27 28 29 30
31 32 33 34 35 36 37 38 39 40
41 42 43 44 45 46 47 48 49 50
51 52 53 54 55 56 57 58 59 60
61 62 63 64 65 66 67 68 69 70
71 72 73 74 75 76

INSTRUCTIONS

FOLD BILLS

INSERT BILLS ONE AT A TIME

INSERT COINS

CLEAR SLOT

USE KEY OR STUFFER

Providence, Rhode Island

TO INTRODUCE

Berlin, Germany

Berlin, Germany

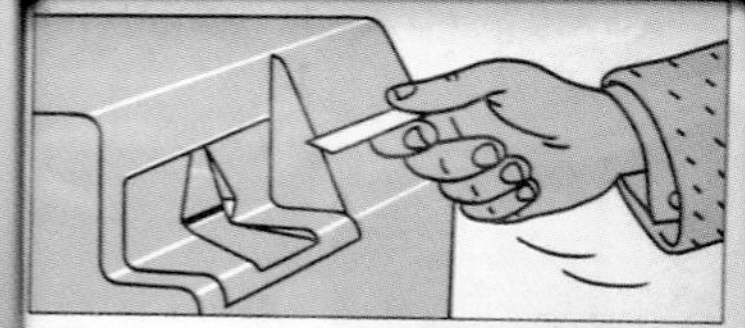
PORTEURS
DE CARTE ORANGE
VOUS DEVEZ VALIDER
VOTRE COUPON.
(ART. 19.)

MAIRIE DE PARIS
STATIONNEMENT
PAYANT
TOUS LES JOURS
DE 9H A 19H
SAUF SAMEDIS, DIMANCHES,
JOURS FERIES ET MOIS D'AOUT
1 € / Heure
Le stationnement est limité à 2 heures
maximum sur le même emplacement.
PAIEMENT PAR
PARIS-CARTE
UNIQUEMENT

En vente dans les bureaux de tabac
Stationnement résidentiel payant
Montant forfaitaire :
0,50 € / jour
possibilité d'abonnement hebdomadaire
PARIS INFO-MAIRIE
tél. 08 2000 75 75
STATIONNEMENT
COURTE DUREE
CARTE
DUREE
CARTE

1. Introduire la carte
2. Choisir la durée.
3. Valider
4. Retirer la carte pour obtenir le ticket.
RESIDENTS
AVEC VIGNETTE "RESIDENT"
CARTE
CARTE

1. Mode résident
2. Introduire la carte
3. Valider
4. Retirer la carte pour obtenir le ticket.
Pour annuler

ABONNEMENT : Appuyer sur le bouton jaune "RESIDENT". Puis appuyer sur
DUREE
Introduire alors la carte
Si le solde de la carte est insuffisant, appuyer sur
CHANGER DE CARTE
au lieu de valider, puis suivre les indications de l'appareil.
EN CAS DE PANNE UTILISER UN AUTRE APPAREIL
DROIT DE STATIONNEMENT EXCLUSIF DE TOUTE GARANTIE

Basel, Switzerland

TO SWIPE

Paris, France

Paris, France

Karten-
telefon

CANCEL

CARD
FULLY

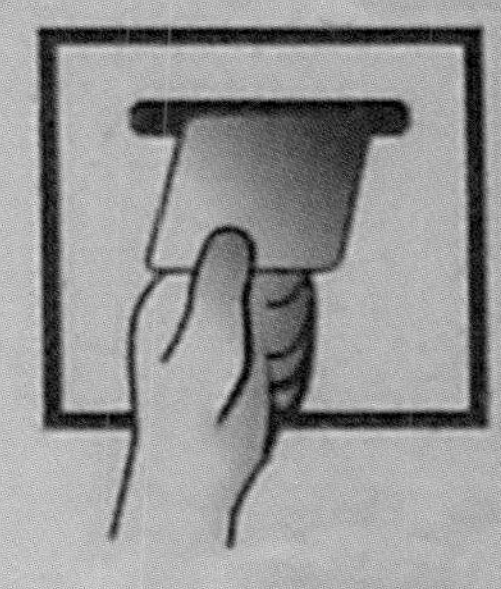

POINT

NSERT
CARD
FULLY
REMOVE
QUICKLY

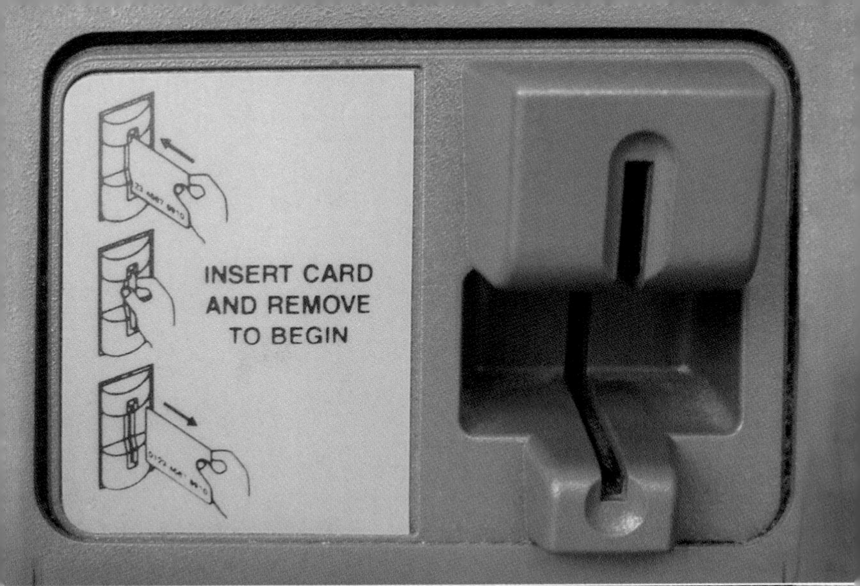

INSERT CARD
AND REMOVE
TO BEGIN

Receipt 
BIENVENIDO
BANK OF AM
WELCOME
BANK OF A

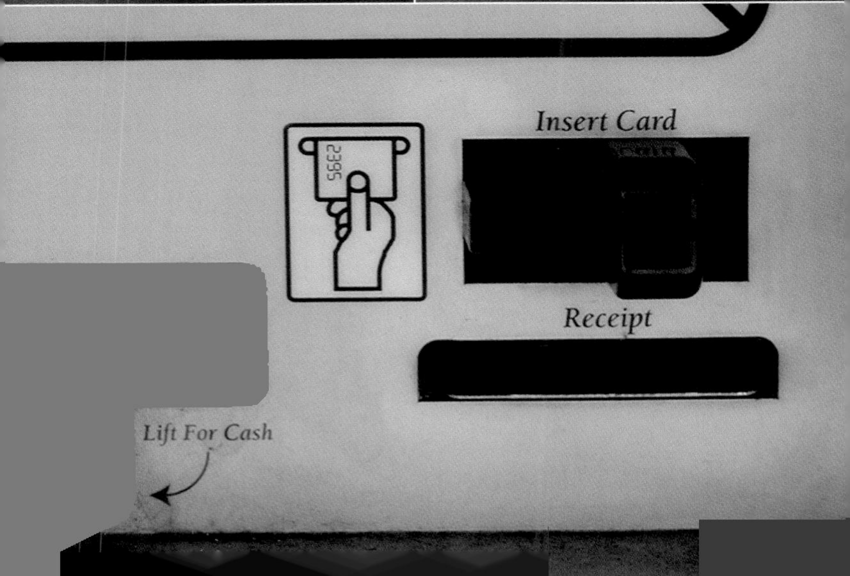

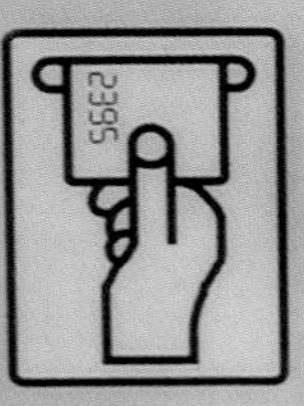

Insert Card

Receipt

Lift For Cash

swipe
card
BANK CARD
1234 5678 9101

Welcome
insert
card
and remove quickly

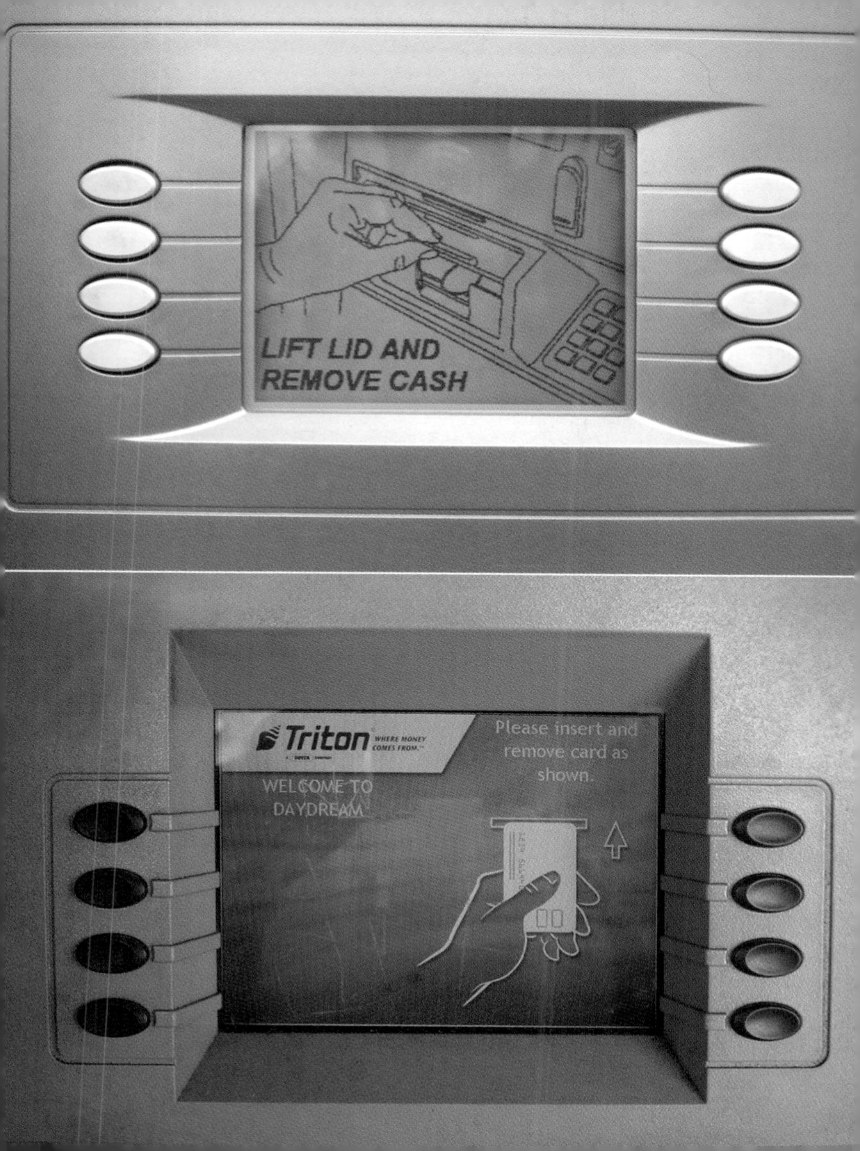

LIFT LID AND
REMOVE CASH
Triton
WHERE MONEY COMES FROM.
Please insert and remove card as shown.
WELCOME TO DAYDREAM

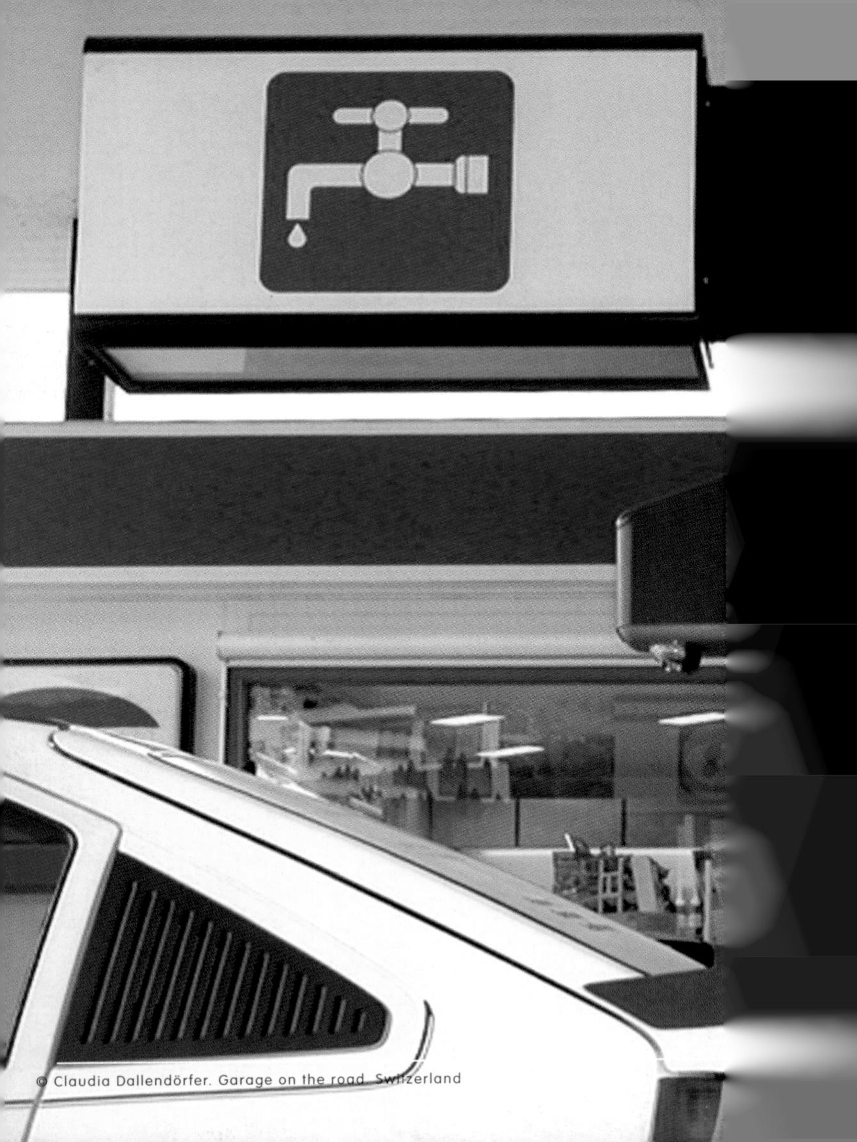

© Claudia Dallendörfer. Garage on the road. Switzerland

Automat
NICHT WARTEN GLEICH PRÜFEN
Diesel
Super Plus 98
TAMOIL

TO TEAR

San Francisco, California

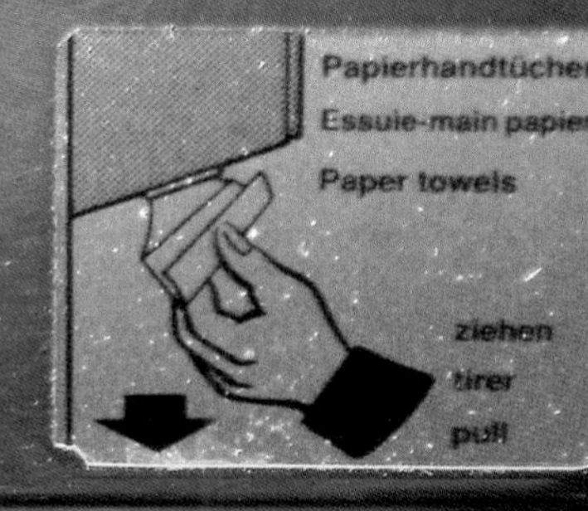

Night train, Switzerland, Germany

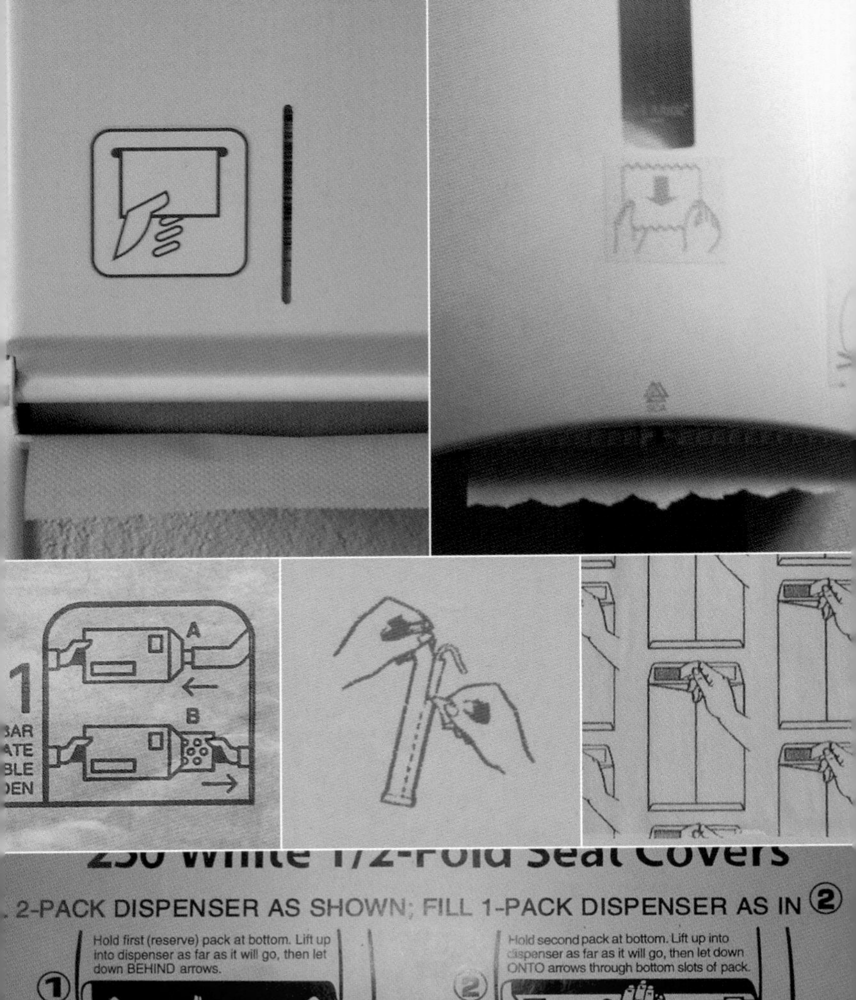
A
B
BAR
ATE
BLE
DEN
250 White 1/2-Fold Seat Covers
2-PACK DISPENSER AS SHOWN; FILL 1-PACK DISPENSER AS IN ②
Hold first (reserve) pack at bottom. Lift up into dispenser as far as it will go, then let down BEHIND arrows.
Hold second pack at bottom. Lift up into dispenser as far as it will go, then let down ONTO arrows through bottom slots of pack.

Pull

If No Paper
Turn Wheel

PULL WITH BOTH HANDS
TIREZ AVEC LES DEUX MAINS
TIRE CON AMBAS MANOS

FORM NO. 033827

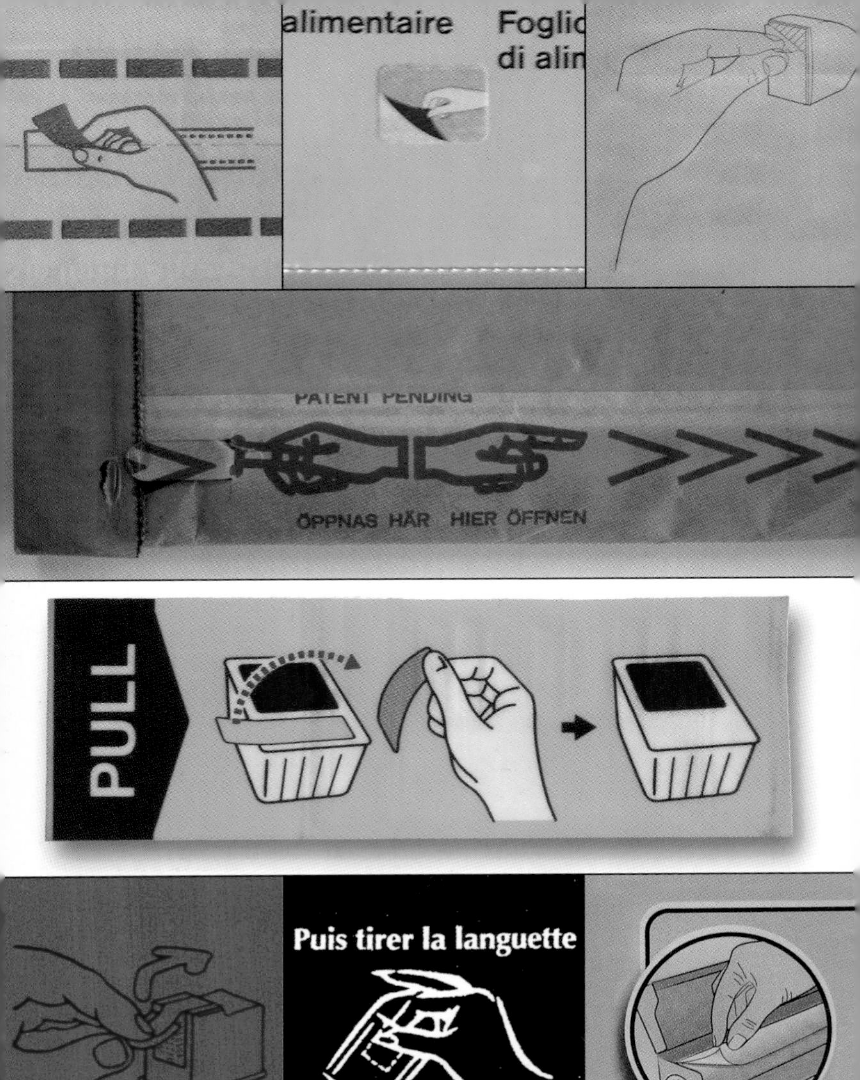
alimentaire
Foglio
di alim
PATENT PENDING
ÖPPNAS HÄR HIER ÖFFNEN
PULL
Puis tirer la languette

1

Insert Fully
Insérer complètement
Introduzca completamente en el chasis
Filmpack vollständig
hineinschieben
奥まで完全に挿入

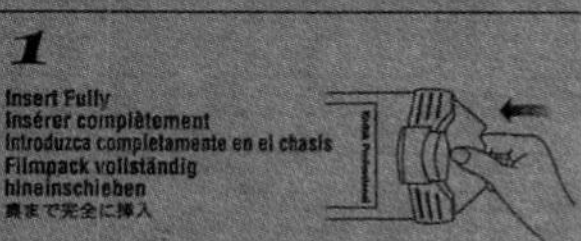

2 Grasp envelope lightly and pull back to stop zone

Saisir l'enveloppe avec précaution et tirer jusqu'à l'indicateur de limite

Tire suavemente del sobre y retírelo hasta la zona de detención.

Filmpack sachte anfassen und bis zum Stoppbereich zurückziehen.

軽く外封をつかみ、停止位置まで引き出す

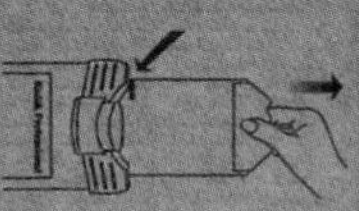

3

Expose
Exposer
Exposición
Belichten
露光

4

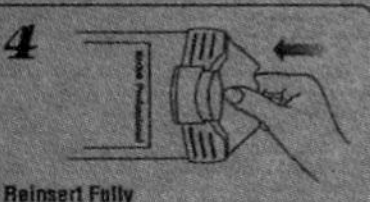

Reinsert Fully
Réinsérer complètement
Reintroduzca completamente en el chasis
Deckblatt wieder hineinschieben
外封を完全に戻す

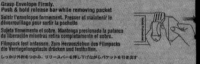

5 Grasp Envelope Firmly.
Push & hold release bar while removing packet

Saisir l'enveloppe fermement. Presser et maintenir le déverrouillage pour sortir la pochette

Sujete firmemente el sobre. Mantenga presionada la palanca de liberación mientras retira completamente el sobre.

Filmpack fest anfassen. Zum Herausziehen des Filmpacks die Verriegelungstaste drücken und festhalten.

しっかり外封をつかみ、リリースバーを押し下げながらパケットを引き出す

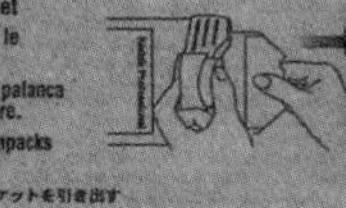

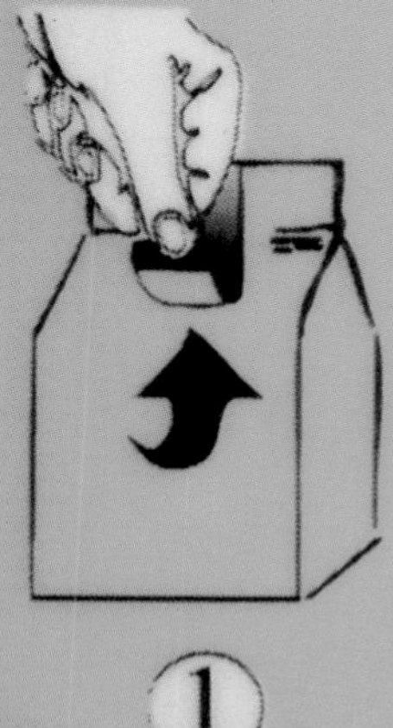

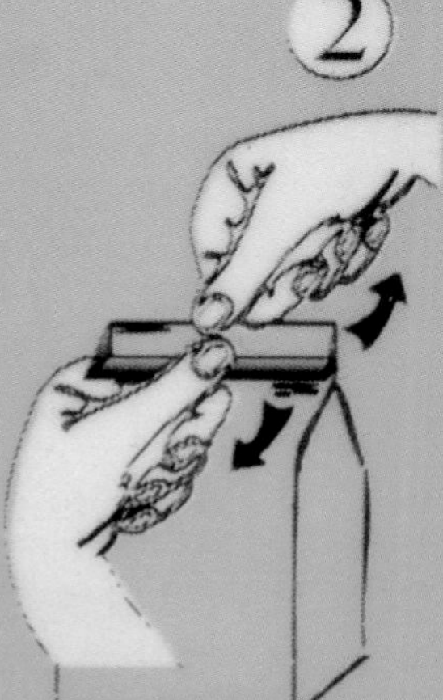

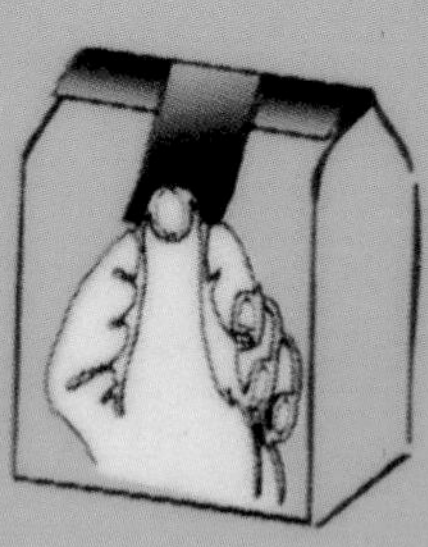

TO PULL

1. LIFT TAB TO RIM. 2. PEEL BACK CAREFULLY.
USE CARE, EDGES MAY BE SHARP.
SOLLEVARE L'ANELLO E PIEGARLO ALL'INDIETRO
LIFT THE RING AND BEND IT BACK
SOULEVER L'ANNEAU ET LE PLIER EN ARRIÈRE
RING LANGSAM SENKRECHT STELLEN
PULL UP PRESSING THUMB ON CENTRE OF
TIRER VERS LE HAUT APPUYANT VOTRE POUCE
MIT DAUMEN AUF DECKELZENTRUM DRÜCKEN UND ABZIEHEN

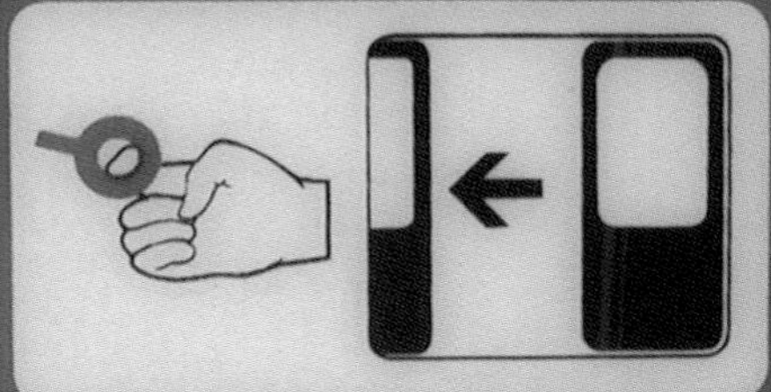
TO OPEN DOORS
IN EMERGENCY
BREAK COVER
AND PULL RING
UIPMENT
EXIT

Train, California

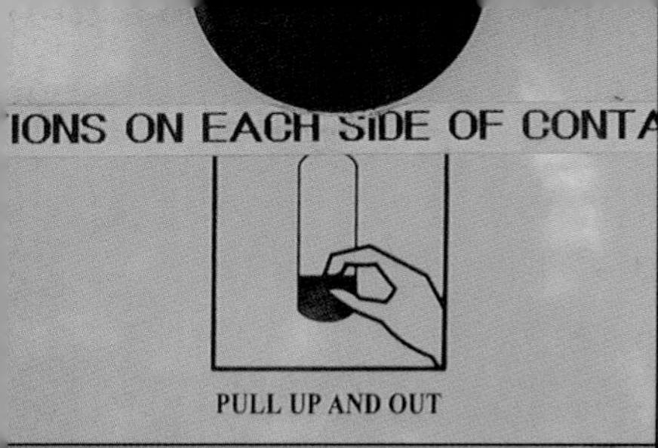

IONS ON EACH SIDE OF CONTA

PULL UP AND OUT

Huntington®
brand

Place fingers un
spout & pull forw

ECOL

PUSH HERE

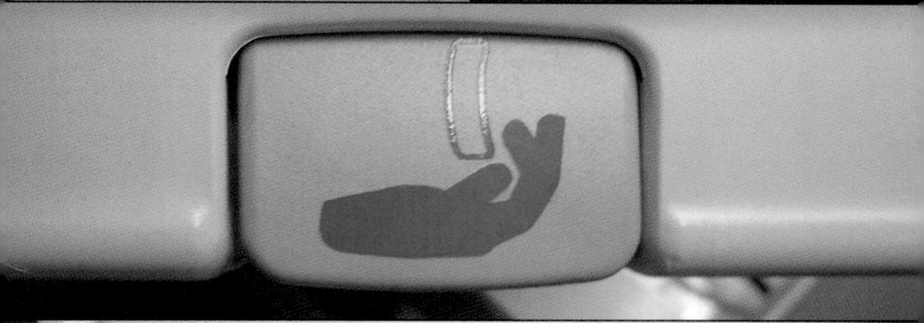

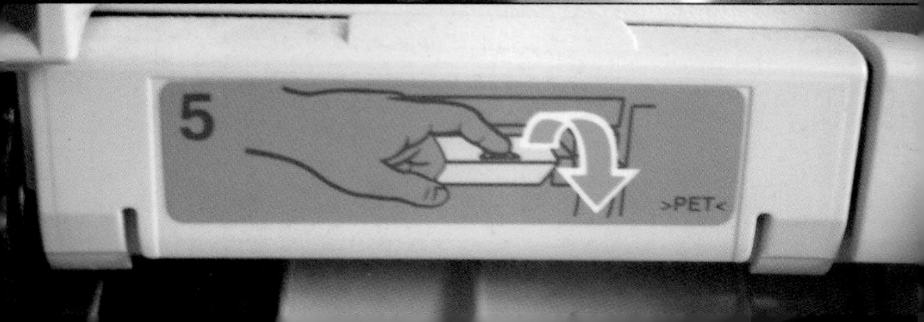

5

>PET<

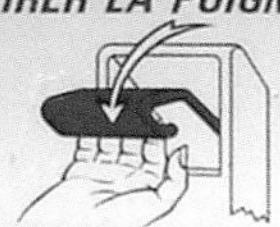

EN CAS DE DANGER
TIRER LA POIGNEE
TOUT ABUS SERA PUNI

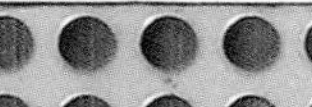
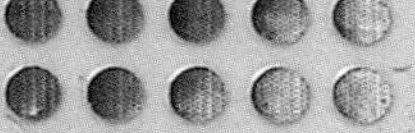
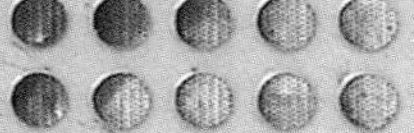

Signal d'alarme
Ne tirer la poignée qu'en cas de danger : tout abus sera puni
For emergency use only : incorrect use will lead to prosecution
Ziehen Sie den Griff nur im Notfall : jeder Mißbrauch wird bestraft
No accionar salvo en caso de peligro : todo abuso sera castigado
Tirare la maniglia solo in caso di pericolo : ogni abuso sara punito

Subway. Paris, France

TO GRIP

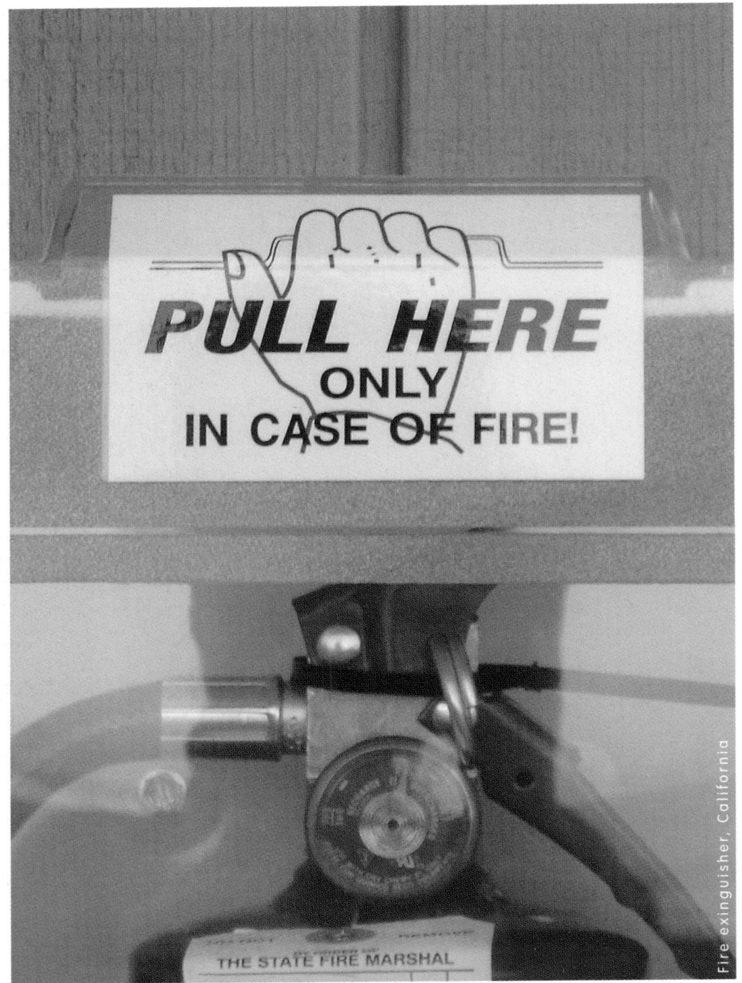

Fire exinguisher, California

Train station, Switzerland

Ask For it By Name....
Smokers' Oasis
EX-CELL
www.smokersoasis.com

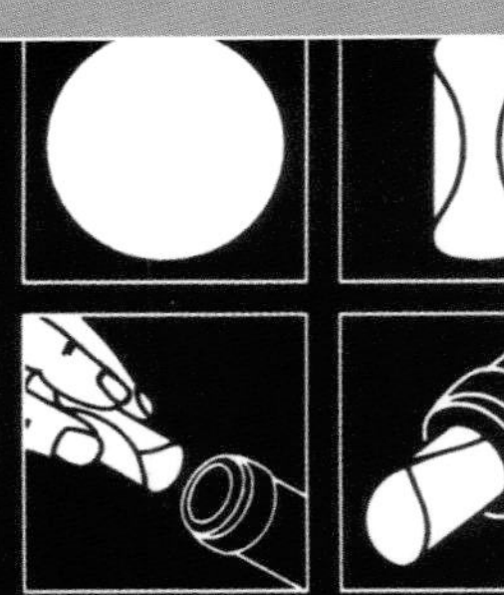

Grandvaux, Switzerland

San Francisco, California

TO THROW

Pacifica, California

San Francisco, California

© Claudia Dallendörfer. On the way to La Chaux-de-Fond, Switzerland

EN PANNE

© Daniel Furon / www.furon.net Graffiti under a bridge, San Pablo Ave, Oakland, California

HAND	GESTURE
HOLD	
TAKE	
ATTACH	 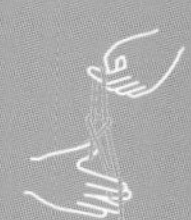
WIPE	
GRIP	

COFFEE
TO THE
PEOPLE

COFFEE
BREAK

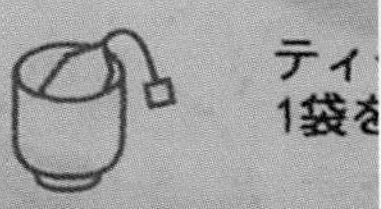

パックを軽く振り
コーヒー粉を下

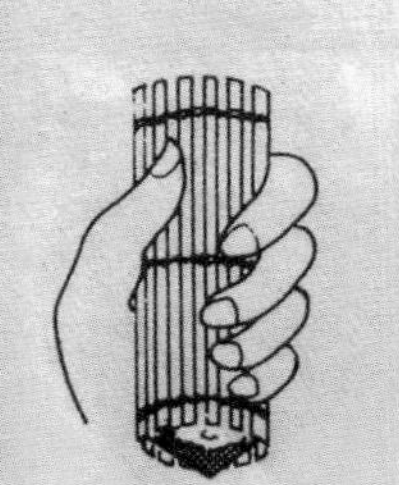
③巻いて締める。

熱湯

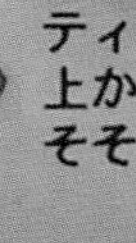

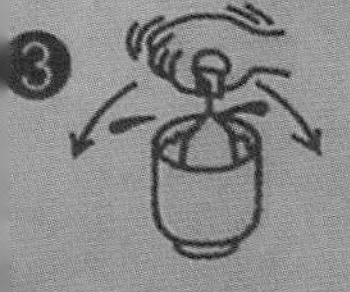

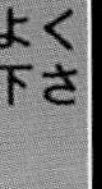

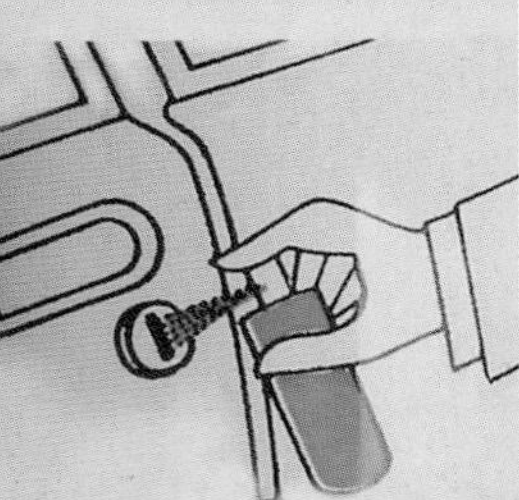

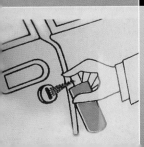

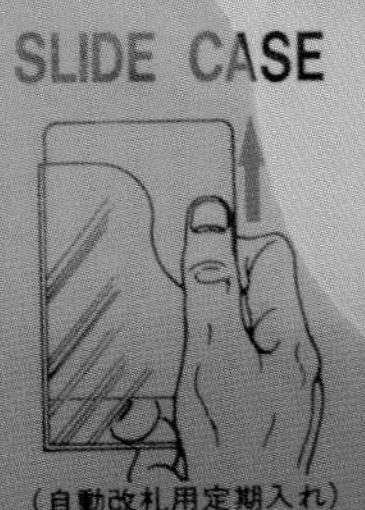
SLIDE CASE
(自動改札用定期入れ)

The Original
Patented

San Francisco

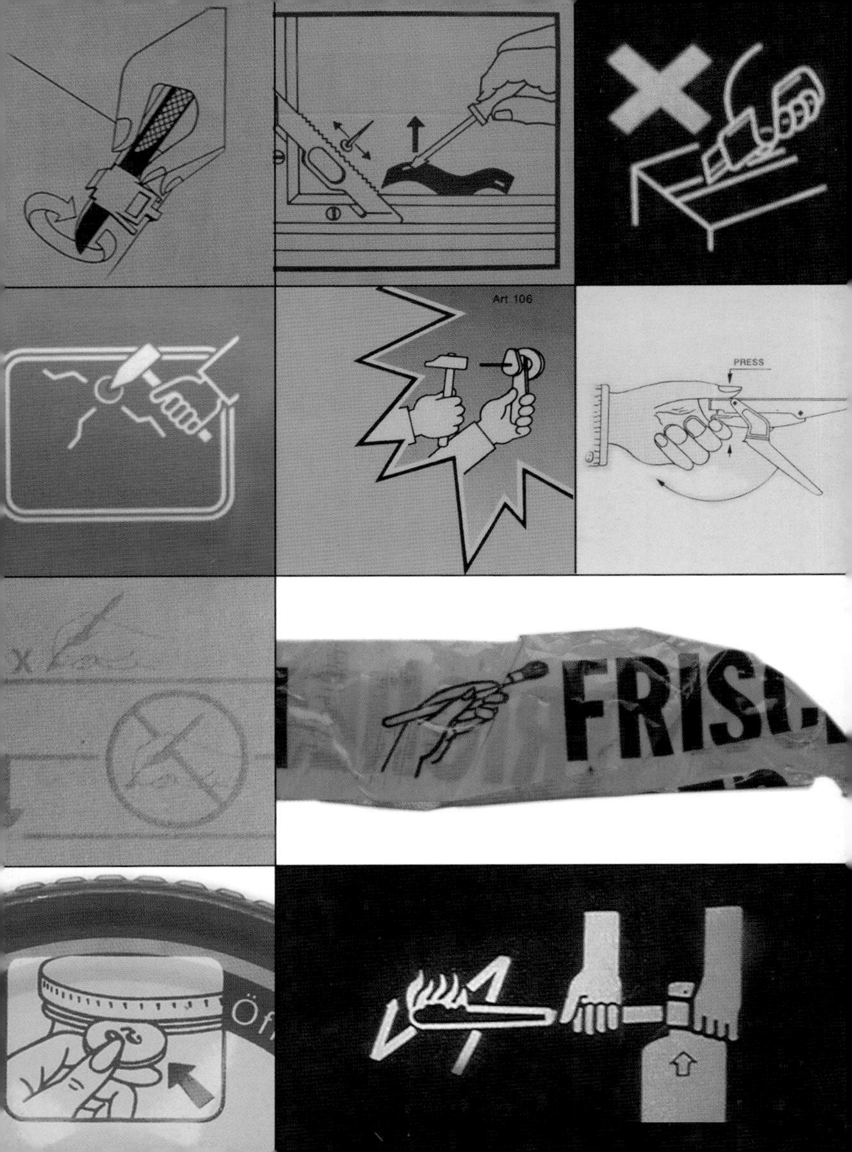
Art. 106
PRESS
FRISC
Öf

OFICIAL

RTIDISTA

NSOLIDADAS

E SAN FRANCISCO

e picture. To vote for a
ete the arrow.

時，

o se indica
rsona

THE VOTERS

Official ballot paper, california

Japantown, San Francisco

Parc, Basel, Switzerland

STOP

1

2

STOP

3

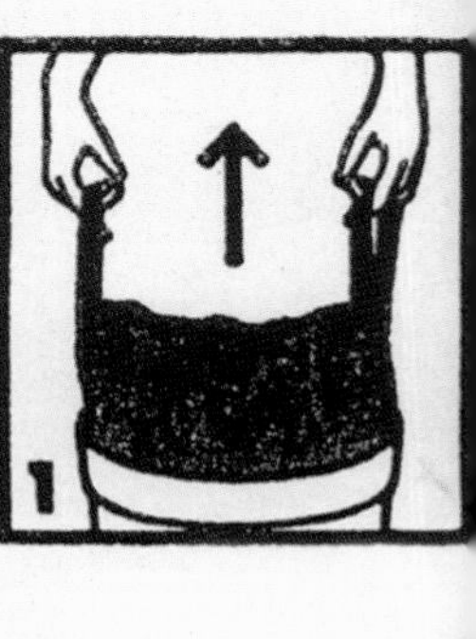

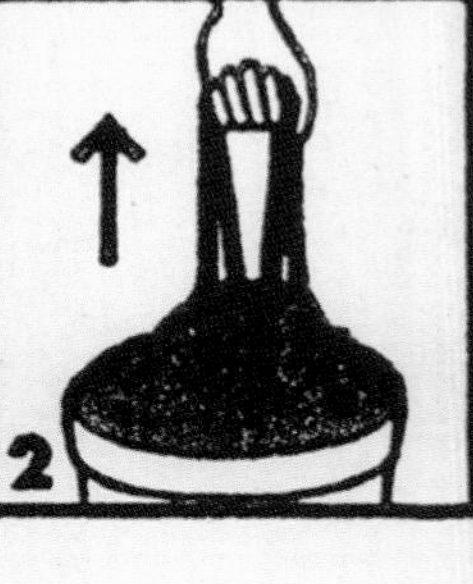

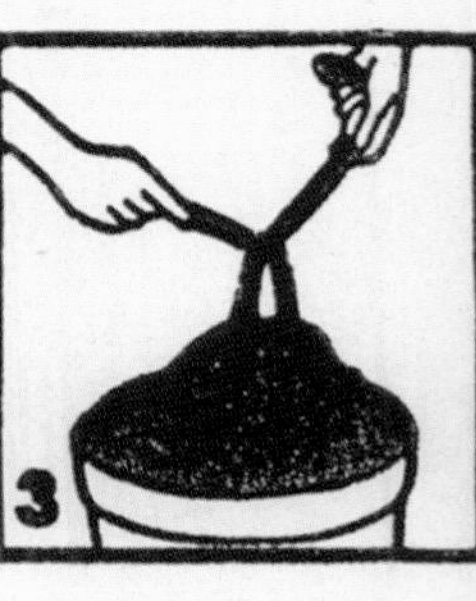

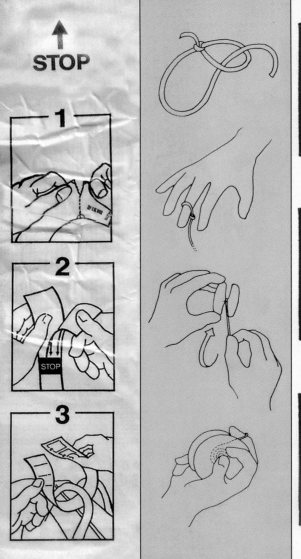

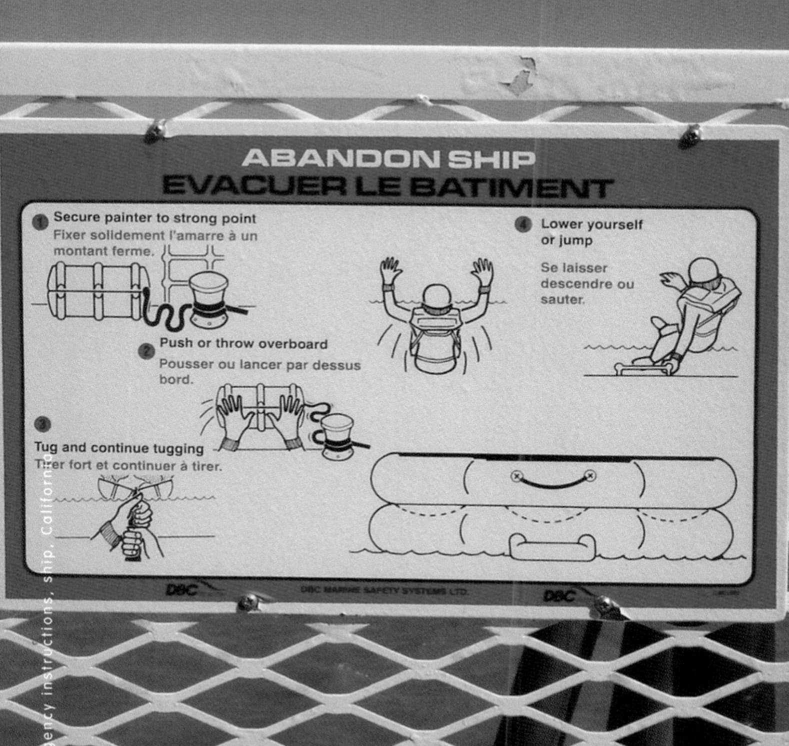

Emergency instructions, ship, California

TO TAKE

Pacifica, California

Garage, Oron, Switzerland

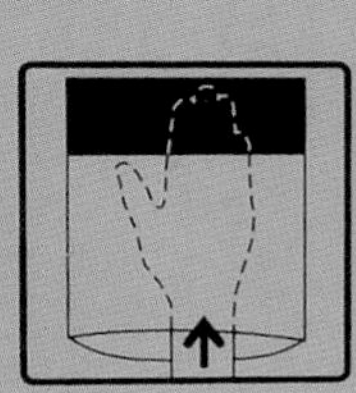

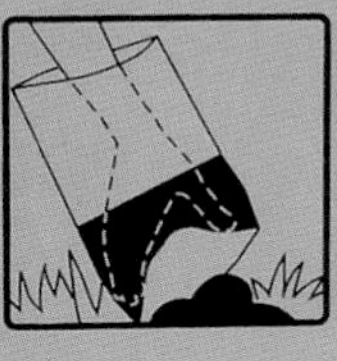

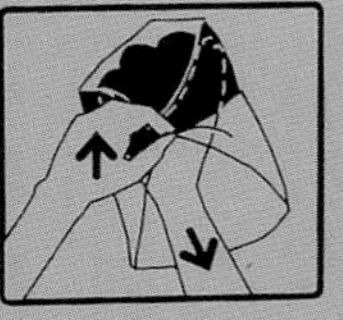

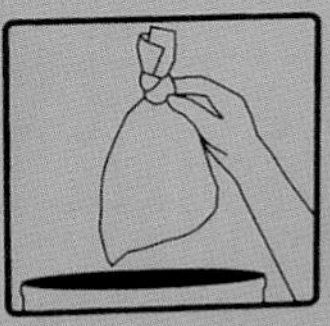
MUTT MITT
Intelligent Products, Inc.
Burlington, Kentucky 41005
800-697-6084
www.pickupmitts.com
© 2001

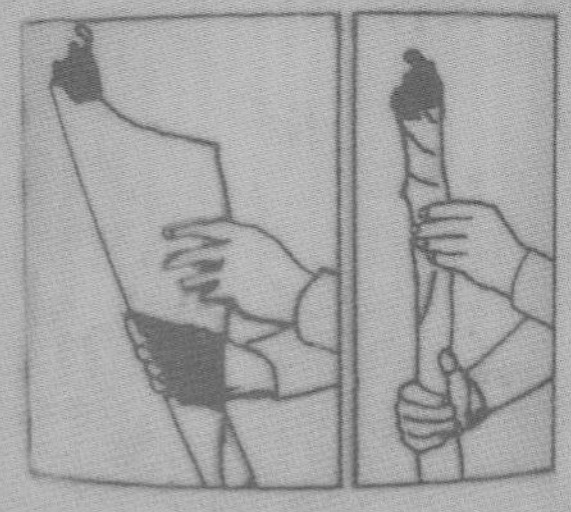

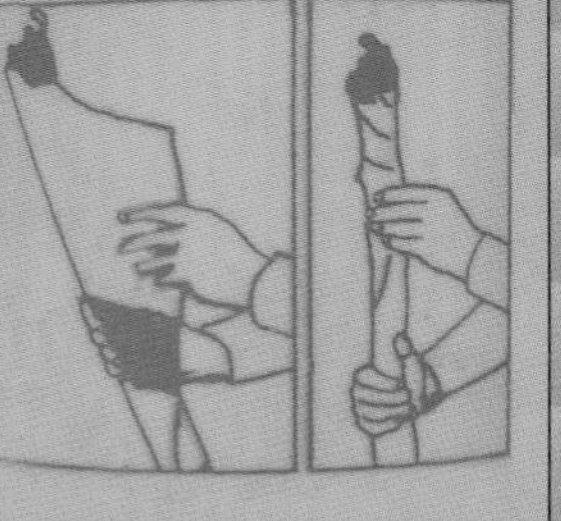

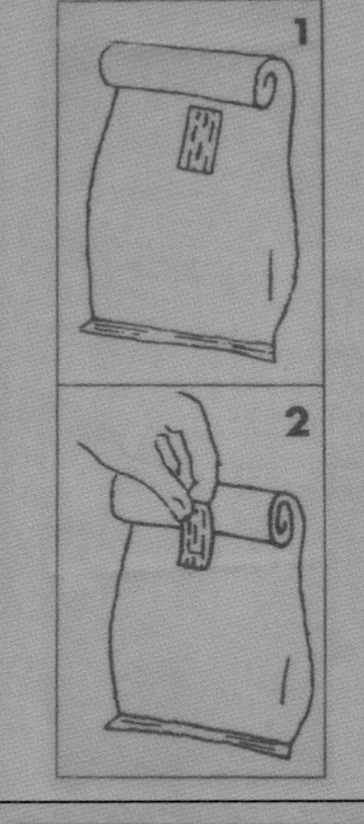
1
2

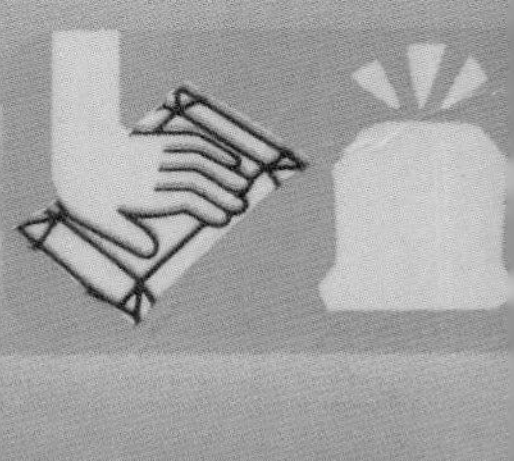

Press'n Seal

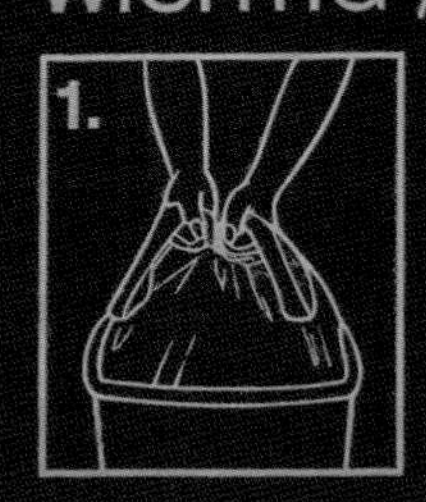
WICHTIG
1.

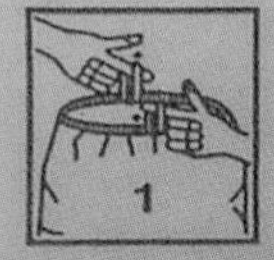
20 Stück pièces pezzi 17
1

2

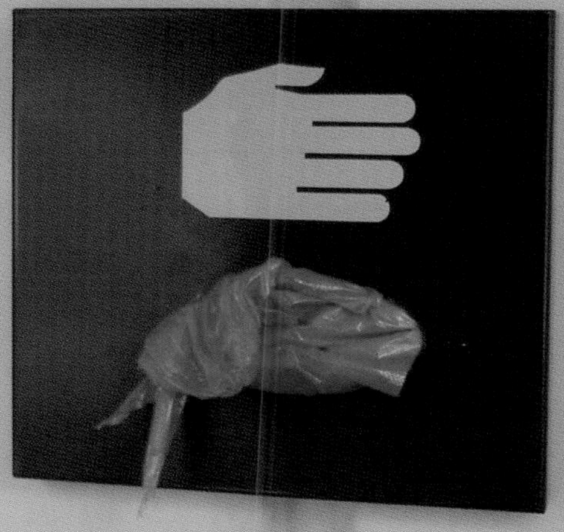

Garage, Balstahl, Switzerland

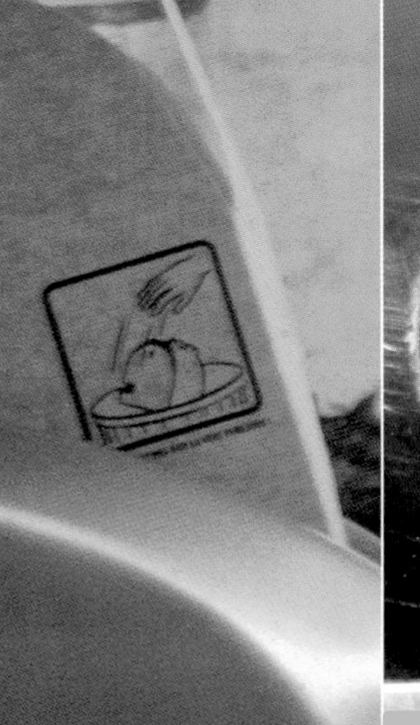

1.

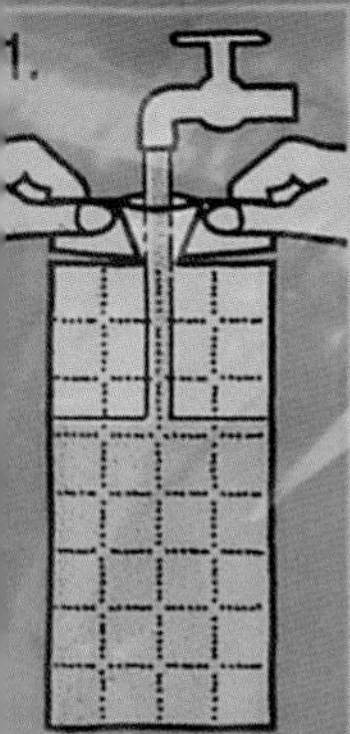

Wasser durch den Trichter einfüllen. Laschen verknoten und Beutel in das Gefrierfach geben.

Remplir le sachet d'eau par l'ouverture supérieure

2.

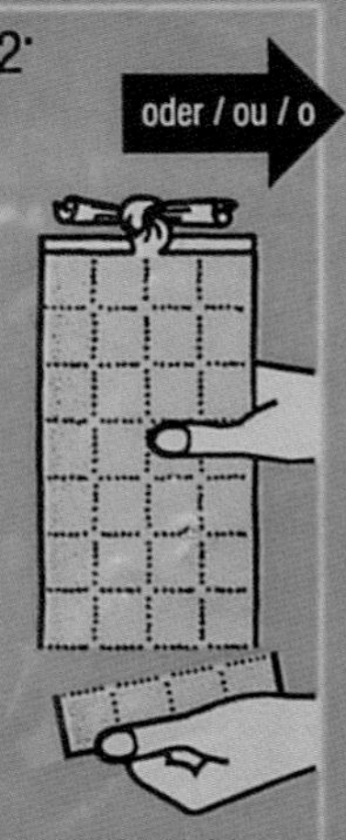

Einzelne Eiswürfel-Reihen entlang der

3.

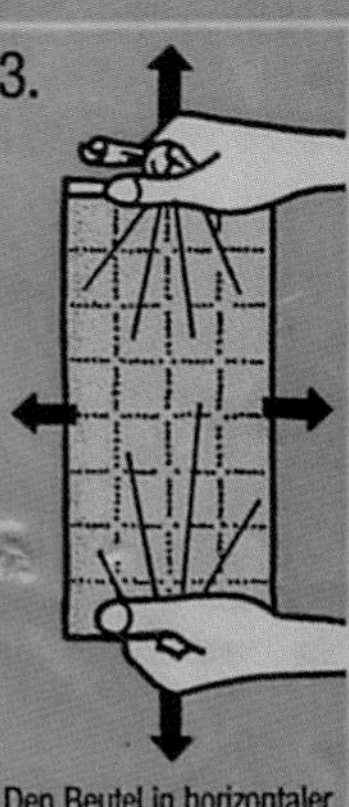

Den Beutel in horizontaler und vertikaler Richtung auseinanderziehen, damit sich die Eiswürfel lösen.

Tirer sur le sachet verticalement et horizon-

4.

Den Beutel öffnen und gewünschte Anzahl Eiswürfel herausnehmen. Kein aufschneiden des Beutels mehr erforderlich.

Ouvrir le sachet et en extraire le nombre de glaçons désirés. Il n'est plus nécessaire de

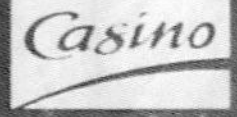

Sac Congélation

Date: Contenu:

Napkins, Mexican restaurant, San Francisco

お湯
軽くしぼる
熱湯
味つけした
①
②
③
④
3 ROLLEN
68 BLATT
ca. 10,2 m PRO ROLLE
2 LAGEN
ca. 15,0 x 25,2 cm BLATTFORMAT
HAUS-HALTS-TÜCHER
ESSUIE-
ROUL-
PAR
DIMENSIONS
•Durable
●ソフトで丈夫、清潔なお台所のキッチン

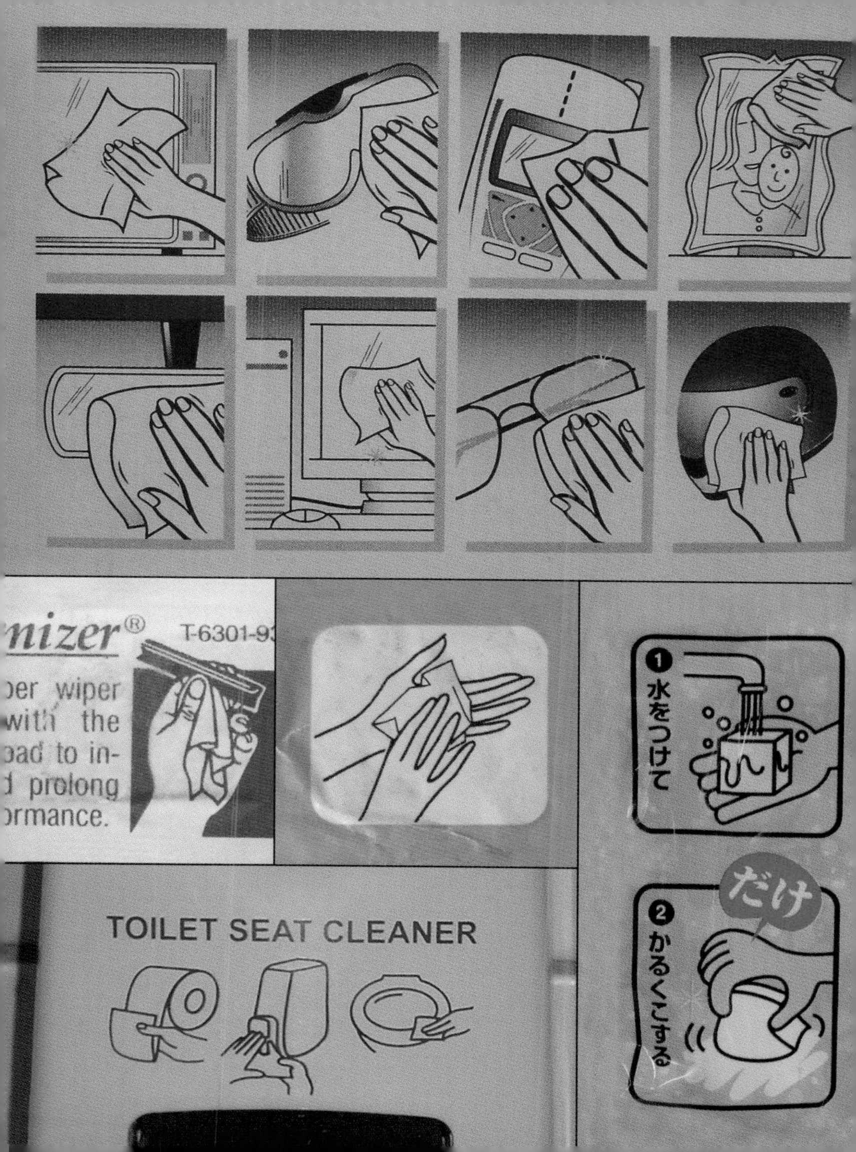

nizer®
T-6301-93
per wiper
with the
pad to in-
d prolong
ormance.

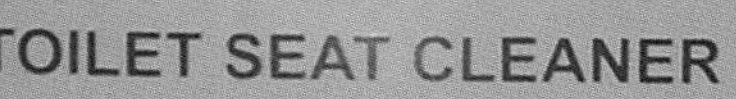

TOILET SEAT CLEANER

1
水をつけて

だけ
2
かるくこする

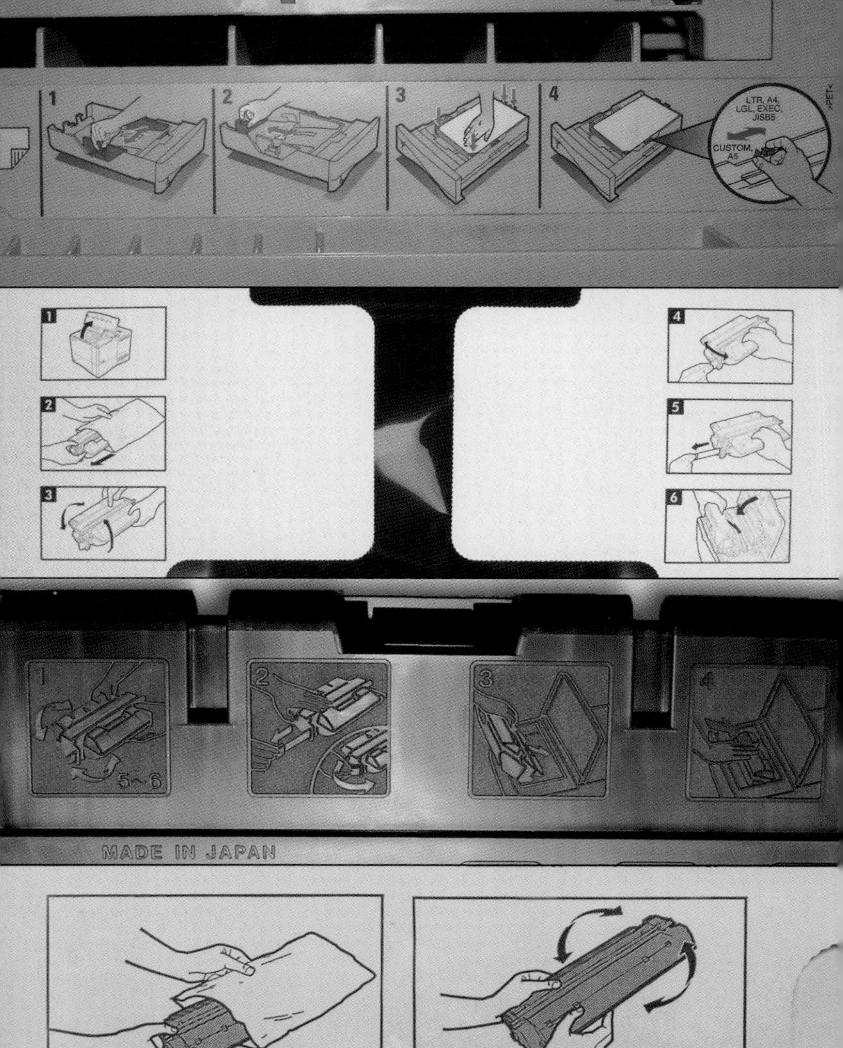

LTR, A4,
LGL, EXEC,
JISB5
CUSTOM,
A5
5~6
MADE IN JAPAN

ECHLICH
5702
HANDLE WITH CARE
TEAM LIFT
FOR YOUR SAFETY...
LIFT BY 2 PERSONS
SKU NO.: 12

Q'TY.: 1

Open here

INFO

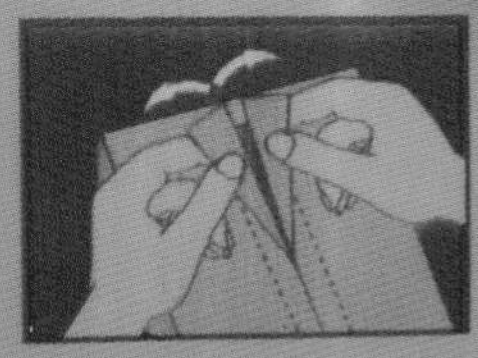

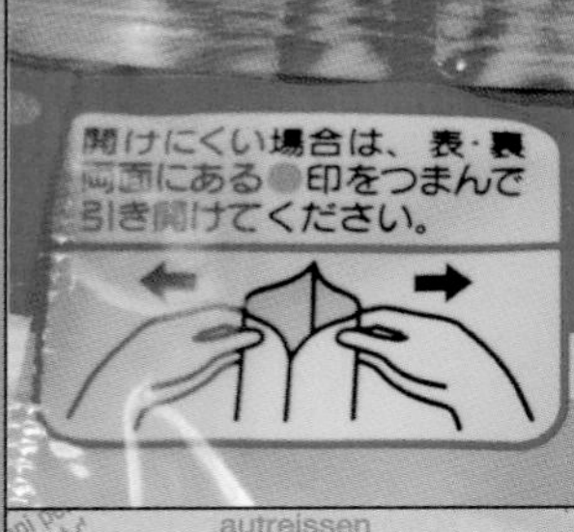

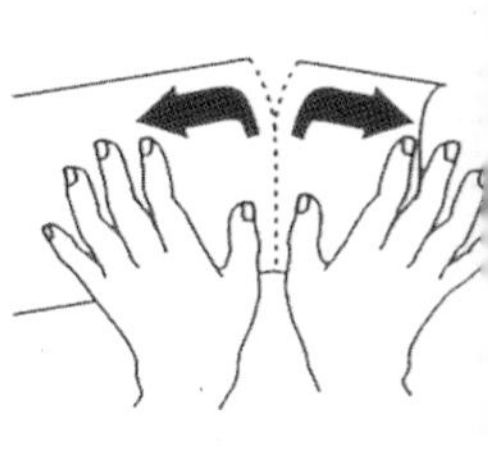

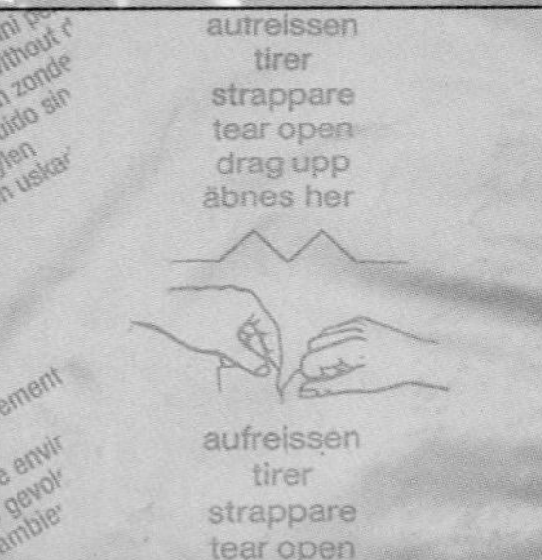

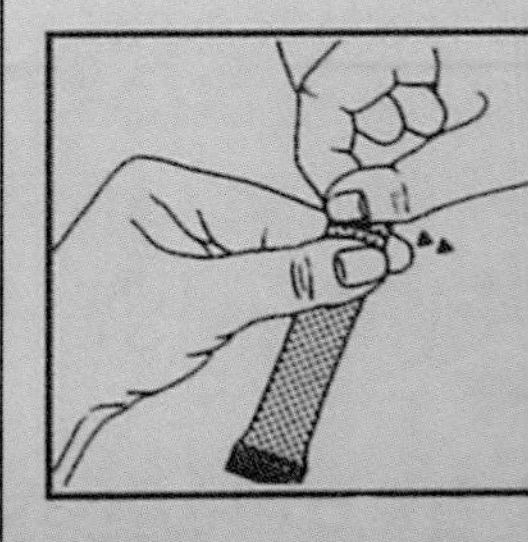

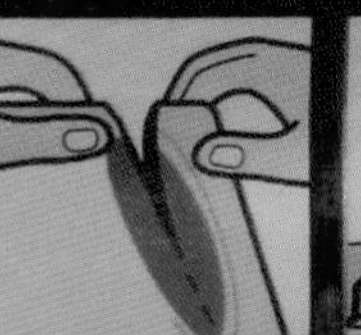

② FOLD WINGS ALL THE WAY BACK UNTIL THEY TOUCH THE CARTON.
③ SQUEEZE SIDES OF WINGS AND PULL FORWARD TO POP OPEN SPOUT.
OPEN
① SEPARATE WINGS.
GRADE A PASTEURIZED
HOMOGENIZED
REDUCED FAT MILK
VITAMIN A & D ADDED
FAT REDUCED FROM 8g TO 5g
PER SERVING
Nutrition Facts
Serving Size 1 Cup (240mL)
Servings Per Container about 4
Amount Per Serving

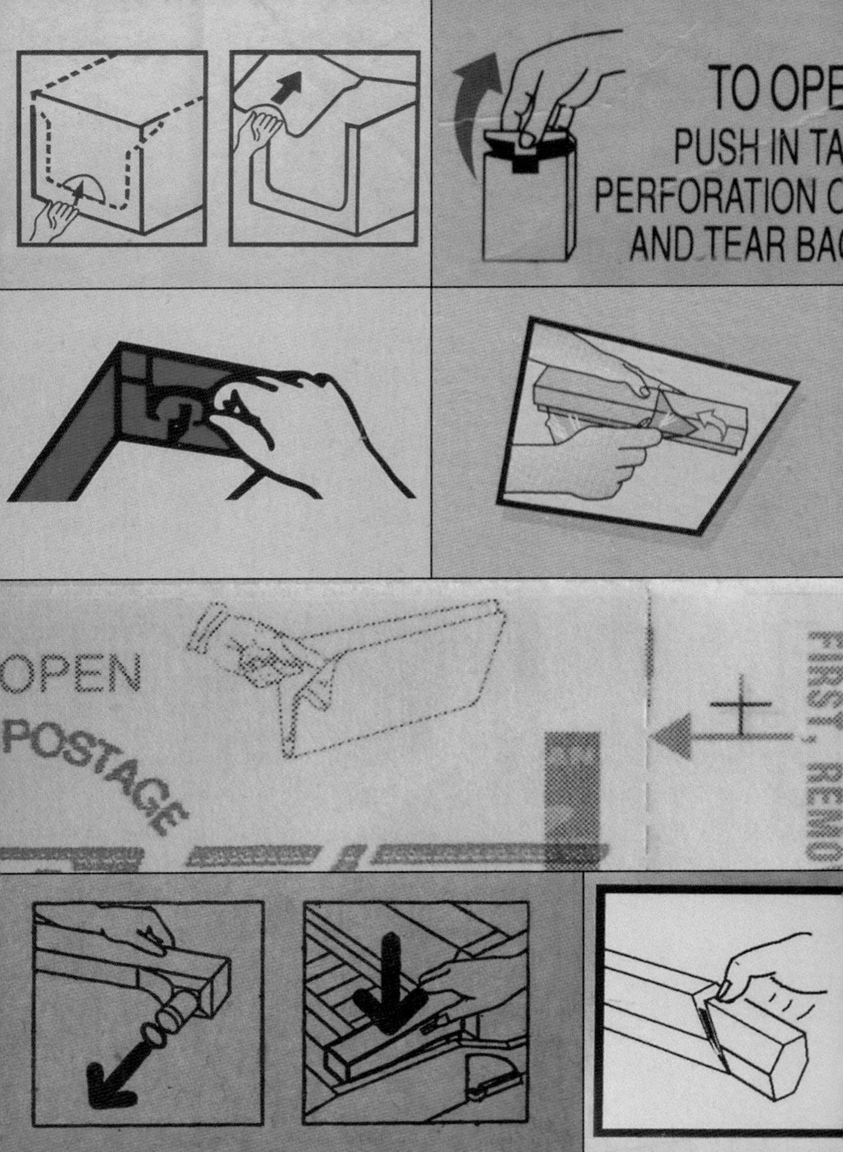
TO OPE
PUSH IN TA
PERFORATION C
AND TEAR BAG
OPEN
POSTAGE

1.
2.

Pass
Ticket
Passkontrolle
Passport Control

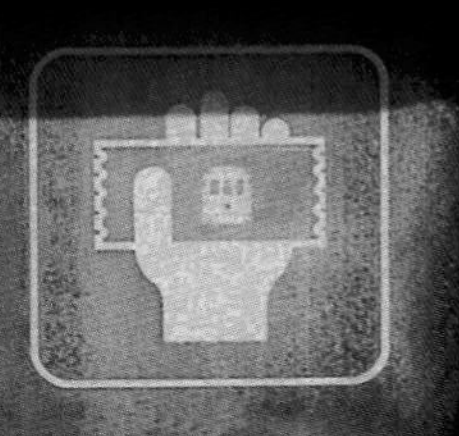
Buy Ticket
Before
Entering
Line

TICKETS
NO tickets sold onboard Caltrain.
Violators may be cited.
Proof-of-Payment
MUST HAVE A VALID
CALTRAIN TICKET
BEFORE BOARDING
• Buy ticket at vending machine.
• NO tickets sold onboard.
• 10-ride tickets must be validated

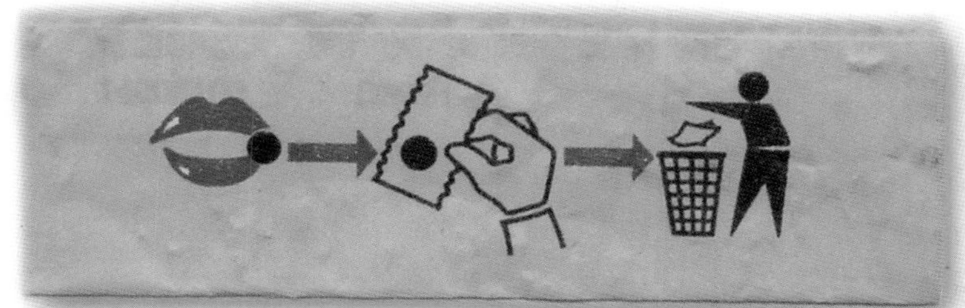
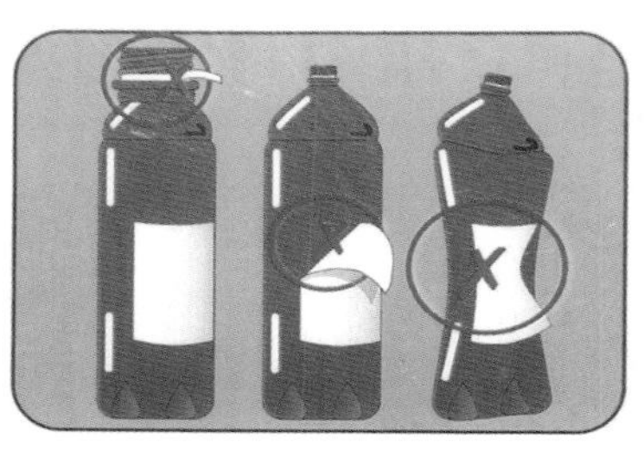
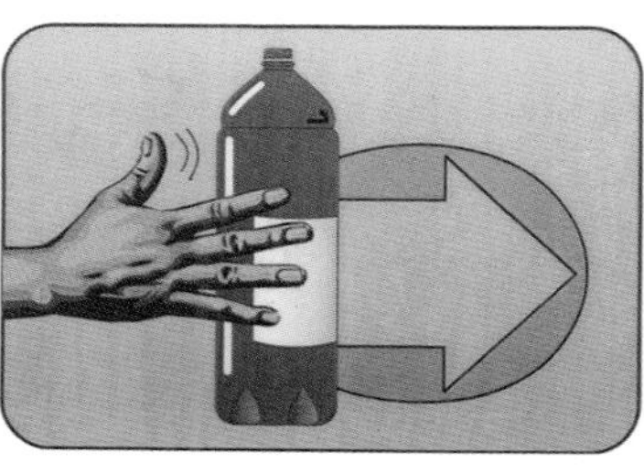

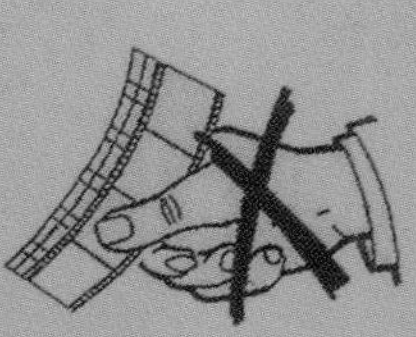

© Joachim Müller-Lancé / www.kamedesign.com.
Sign at the train station of Hakata, Japan, advertising the upstairs shopping mall.

多デイトス

と情報の街

© Studio AND. Office of found objects. Railway Station, Basel Switzerland

HAND

ICON

DECORATION

REPRESENTATION

ILLUSTRATION

TRANSLATION

INTERDICTION

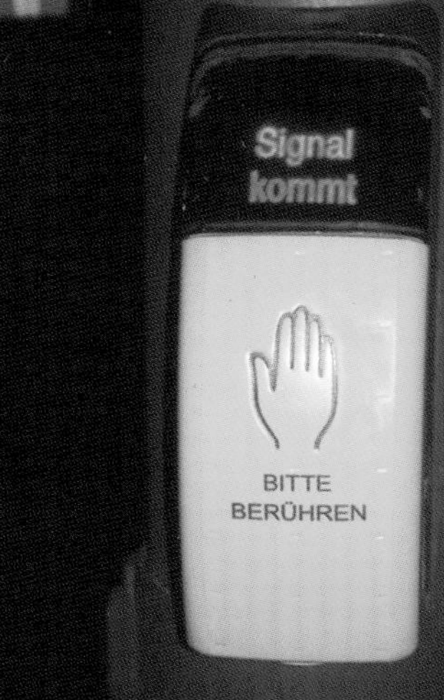
Signal
kommt
BITTE
BERÜHREN

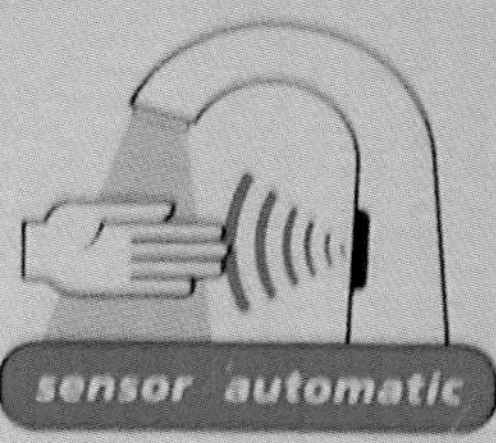
sensor automatic

Motion Activated

Sweatshirt, Dolce & Gabbana

Game on children park, San Francisco, California

Hair dresser window, California

Store, San Francisco

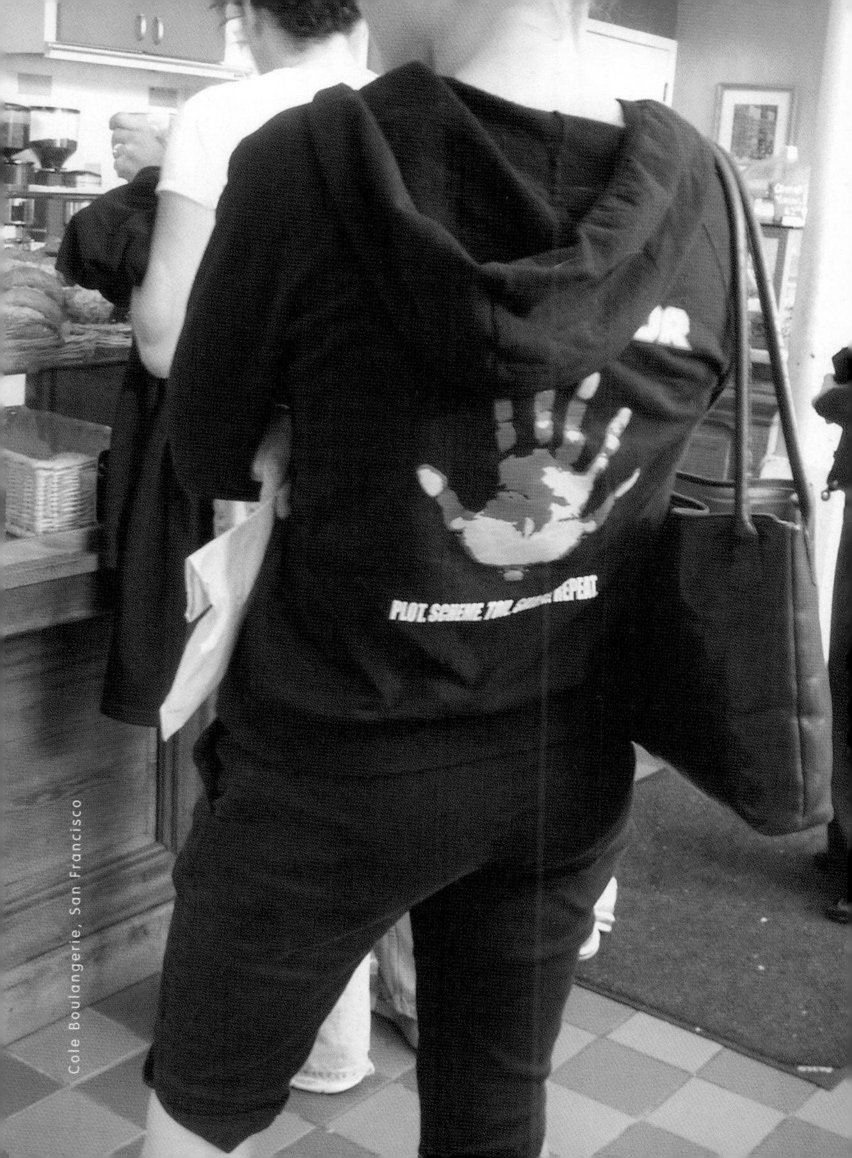
PLOT. SCHEME. TOIL.
REPEAT.

Cole Boulangerie, San Francisco

TO ILLUSTRATE

San Francisco, California

Window decoration, Phoenix Books, California

asts
neu
Ausnahmen:
asler Zeitung
elbe Seiten
HANDLE WITH CARE
TM
FOODSERVICE

Customized licence plate, California

© Jean-Benoît Lévy / Clean Force, hand soap dispenser, Highway 1, California

CLEAN
FORCE
Hand Soap

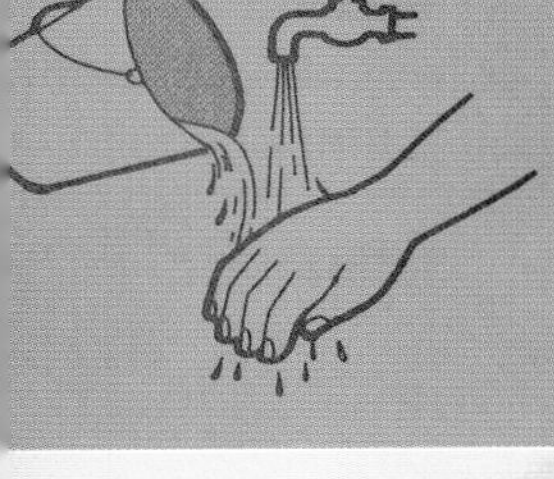

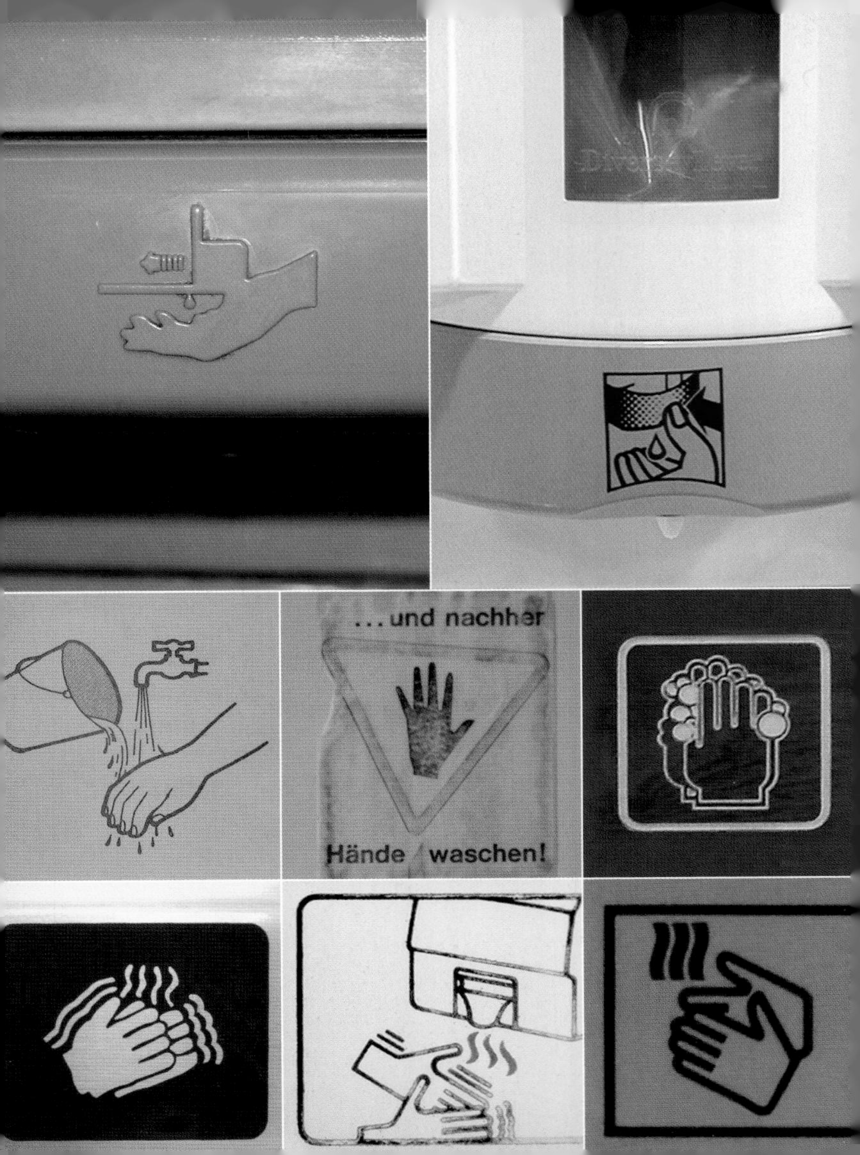

... und nachher

Hände waschen!

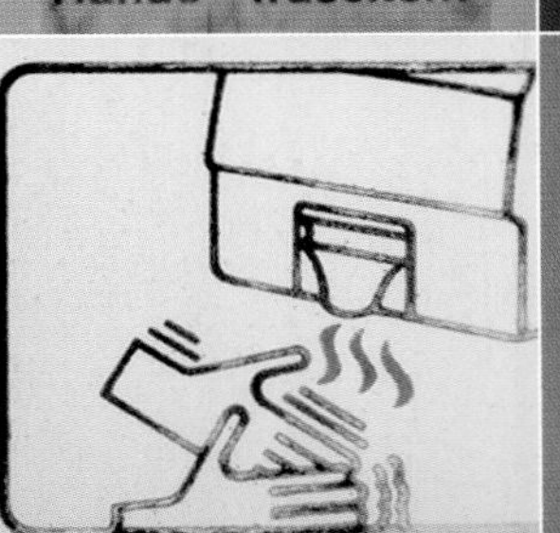

Employees Must
Wash Hands
Before Returning
to Work

1. Wet

2. Soap

3. Wash
for 20 sec.

4. Rinse
5. Dry

6. Turn Off Water
with paper towel

Paper towels box, [illegible]aurant, California

WASH YOUR HANDS
PROTECT THE HEALTH OF OTHERS
AVESE LAS MANO
•BEFORE HANDLING FOOD
•AFTER USING THE RESTROOM
(HEALTH AND SAFETY CODE SECTION 28625-28291)

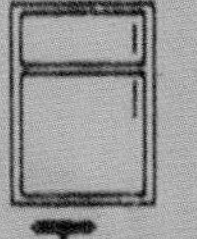
SOME FOOD PRODUCTS M
PRODUCT IS MISHANDLED
THESE SAFE HANDLING INS
KEEP REFRIGERATE
THAW IN REFRIGER

KEEP RAW MEAT
FROM OTHER FO
BOARDS), UTENS

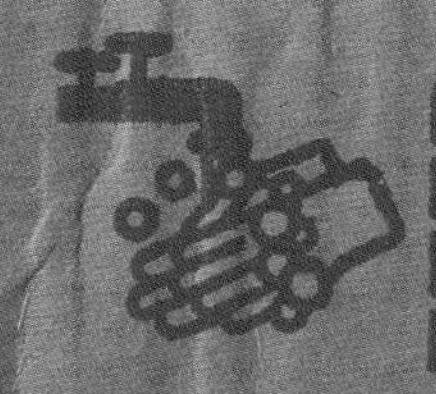
ZEN. THAW IN
VE.
KEEP RAW MEAT AND P
FOODS. WASH WORKIN
BOARDS), UTENSILS, A
MEAT OR POULTRY.

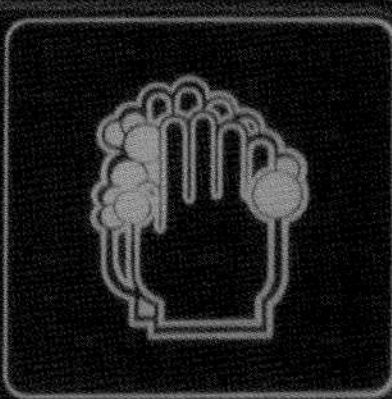
Employees Must Wash
Hands Before Returning
to Work

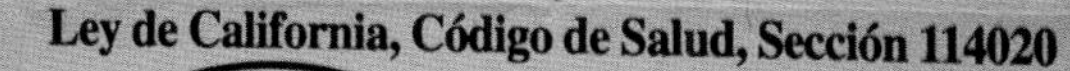
Ley de California, Código de Salud, Sección 114020

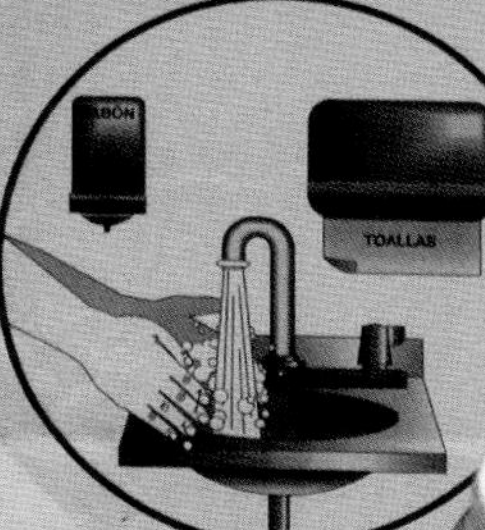
TOALLAS
Los Trabajadores
Deben Lavarse Las Manos
Frecuentemente:
Antes de:
Empezar a Trabajar
Después de:
Usar el baño
Toser o estornudar
Tocar o coger comida cruda
Fumar cigarrillos
Comer o beber
9/00

WASHING IS CRUCIAL
microorganisms
ss contamination
bacterial transfer
ood borne illness
rocessed foods shelf life
Safety Sanitation Program
JARDIAN

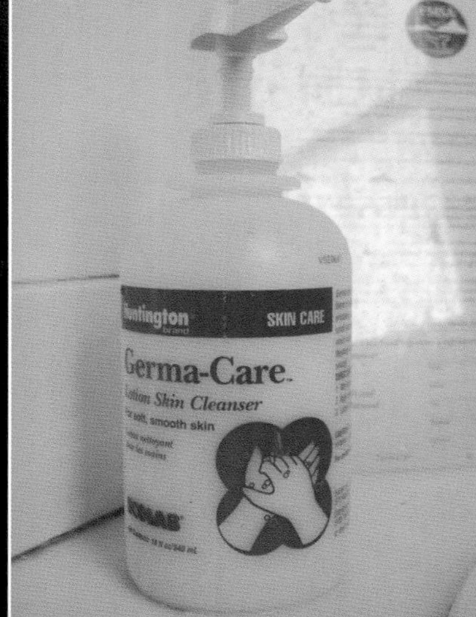
SKIN CARE
Germa-Care
Lotion Skin Cleanser
soft, smooth skin

WASH YOUR HANDS
1
Make lather with soap and water
2
Rub palms, back of hands, and between fingers
3
Rub for 15 seconds
4
Rinse and dry well
Infection:
www.publichealth.va.gov/InfectionDontPassItOn
Department of Veterans Affairs

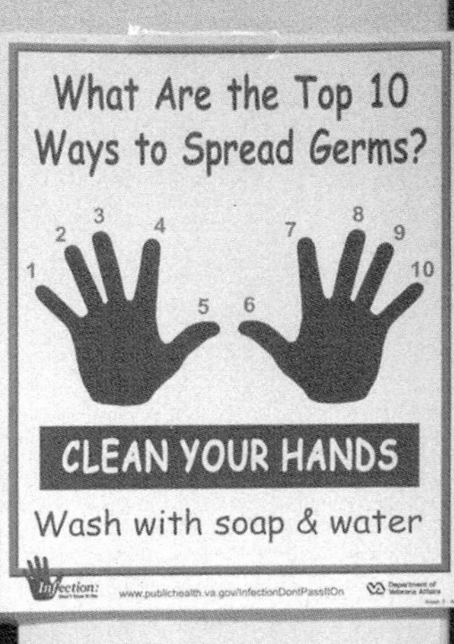
What Are the Top 10 Ways to Spread Germs?
1 2 3 4 5 6 7 8 9 10
CLEAN YOUR HANDS
Wash with soap & water
Infection:
www.publichealth.va.gov/InfectionDontPassItOn
Department of Veterans Affairs

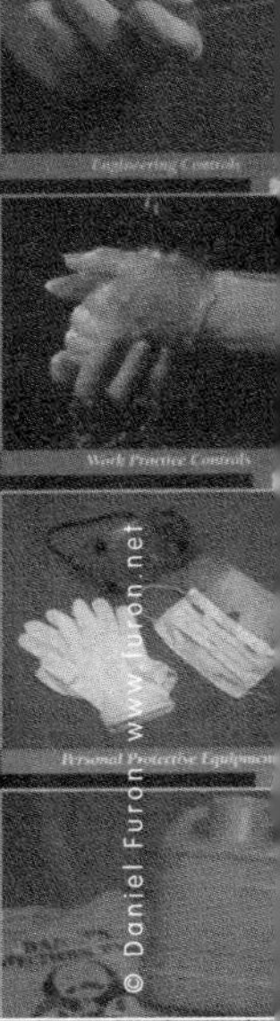
Engineering Controls
Work Practice Controls
Personal Protective Equipment

GB-31

Tücher mit Öffnung nach unten in den Dispenser einlegen.
Poser les feuilles avec l'ouverture tournée vers le bas.
Posare i fogli con l'apertura rivolta verso il basso.

Tela Resart
Handtücher/Essuie-mains
Asciugamani

WASH 'EM
LÁVESELAS
Dirty hands spread DISEASE
Manos sucias desparraman ENFERMEDADES
MARICOPA COUNTY ENVIRONMENTAL SERVICES DEPT
DEPARTAMENTO DE SERVICIOS AMBIENTAL DEL CONDADO MARICOPA

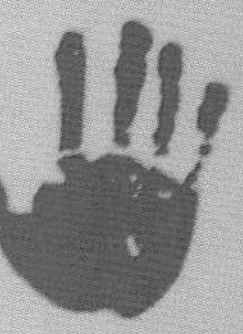

5 STEPS TO PROPER HAND WASHING

Wet hands with water

Apply Hand Wash

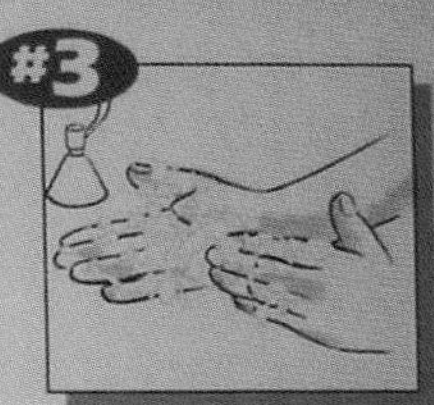

Lather and wash for <u>at least</u> 15 seconds

Rinse both sides of hands with water

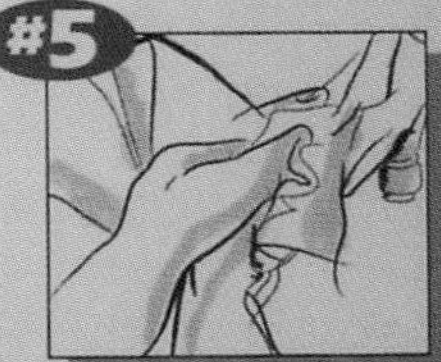

Dry hands and shut off faucet with hand towel

HENNA

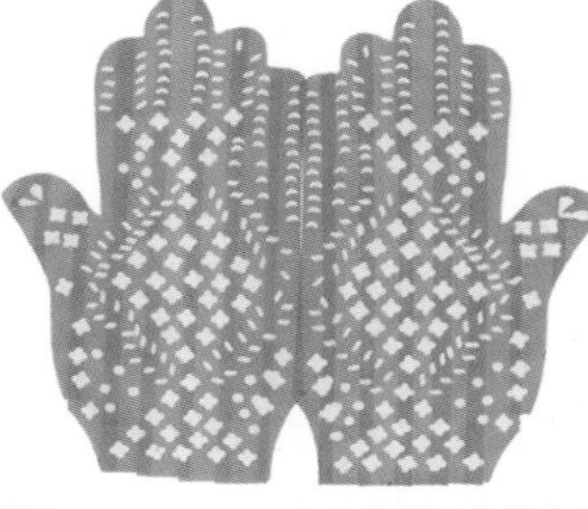

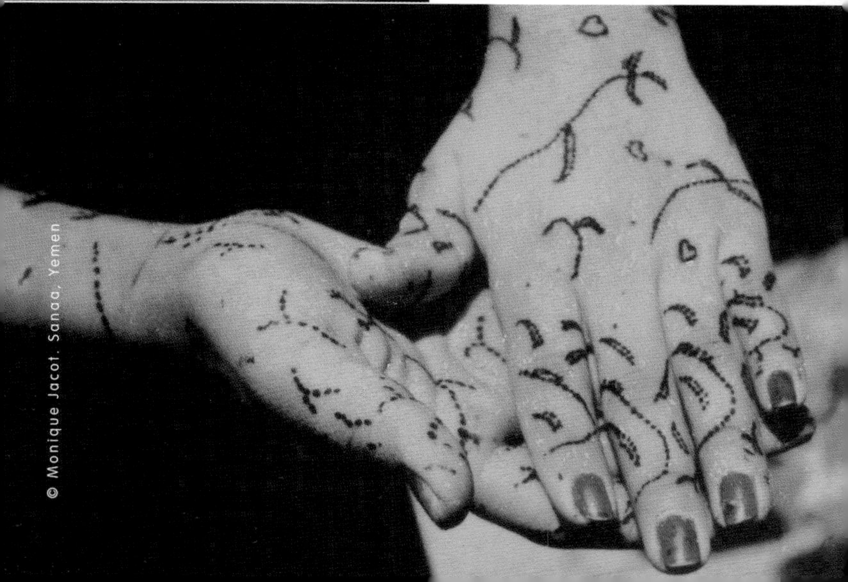

Paris, France

Pedicure salon, California

Rosa, California

WORLD
SECURITY
nirvana
NA
AIRBRUS
DESIG
MA
SSEMBLY
rtificates
ELECT
LILLIAN
SING
郭麗蓮
DEMO

Nail salon, California

© Terry Green / twenty2product. www.twenty2.com. Flowershop in San Francisco.

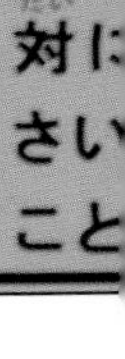

あぶないから
はいっては
いけません

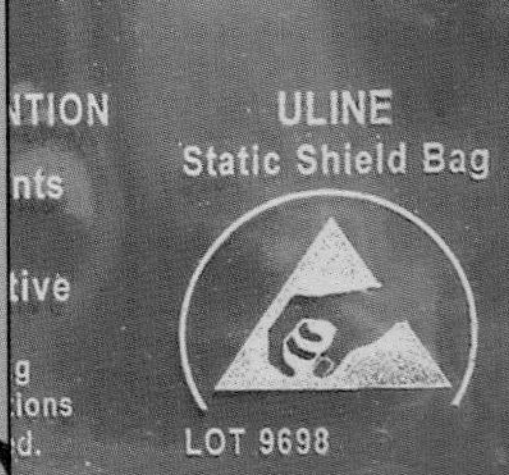
ULINE
Static Shield Bag
LOT 9698

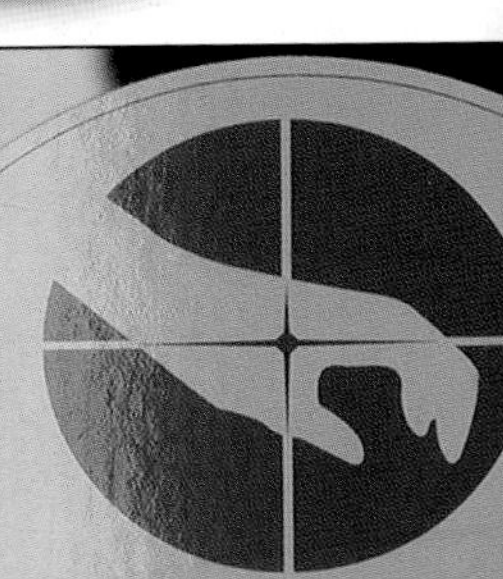

ATTENTION
Contents
Static Sensitive
Handling
Precautions Required
Contents
JEDEC-14/Symbol
S-7607, ULINE, 1-800-295-5510
WORLD CAN'T WAI
DRIVE OUT
HE BUSH REGIME!
OBILIZE FOR NOVEMBER 2, 2005
WWW.WORLDCANTWAIT.ORG

Bern, Switzerland

Lausanne, Switzerland

Elevator, California

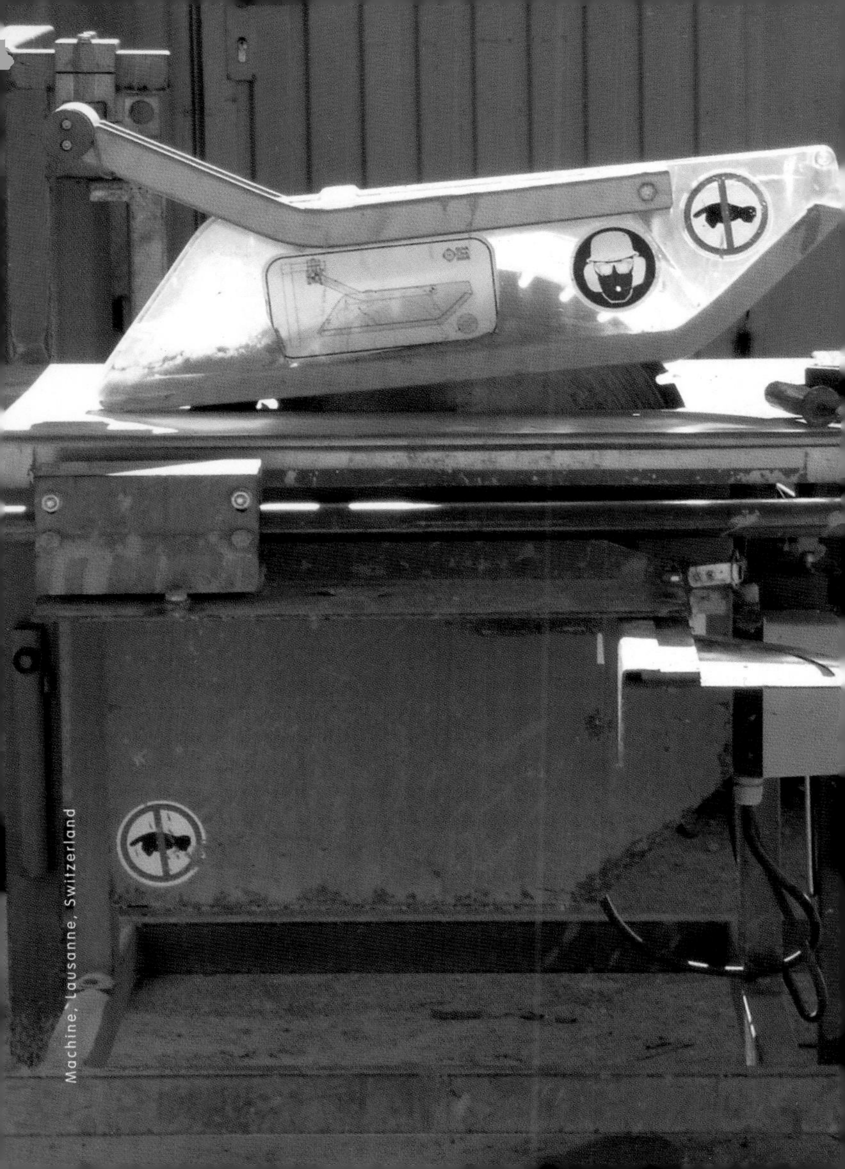

Machine, Lausanne, Switzerland

EXTRAVA

WARNING
KEEP HANDS & CHILDREN CLEAR OF BELT

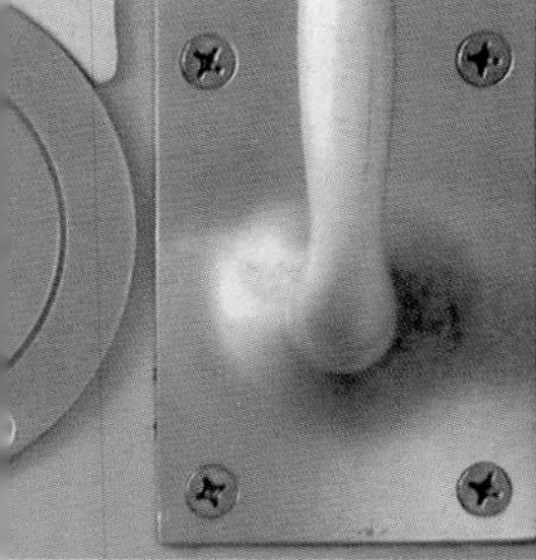

! WARNING
ATCH YOUR
HANDS
AND
FINGERS

AUTION
place your finger on the hinge.
⚠ ATTEN
Ne pas mettre le

かけ込み危
Don't Run

HAND
HAZARD!
Watch your fingers

Ferryboat, San Francisco bay, California

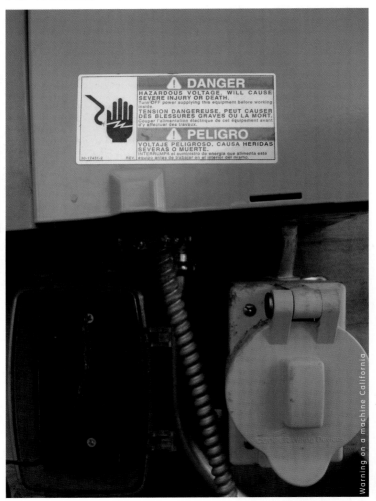

Warning on a machine California

Warning on electric fence, Santa Rosa, California

© Jean-Benoît Lévy / On the railroad between San Jose and San Francisco, California

"ELECTRIC"
THIRD RAIL
DANGER
PELIGRO
KEEP AWAY
NO PASE

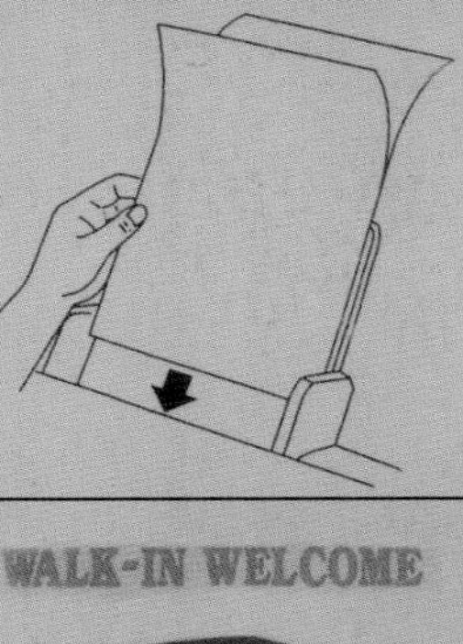
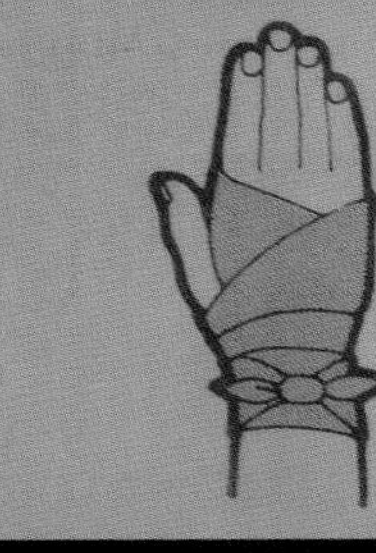

WALK-IN WELCOME
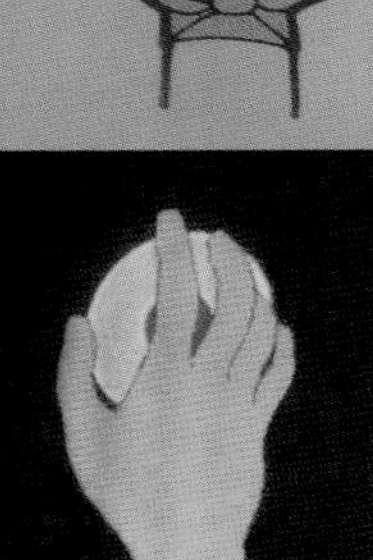

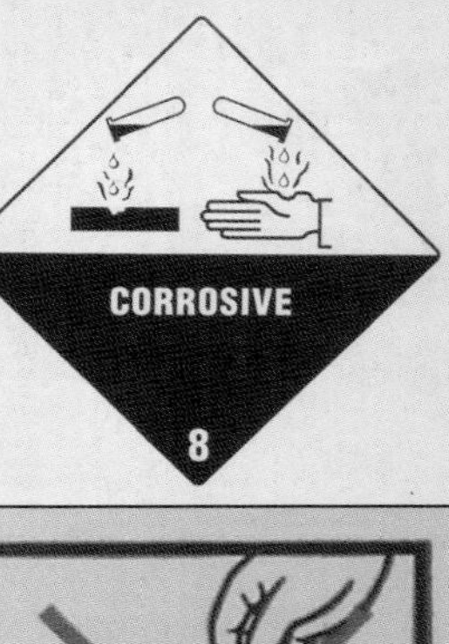
CORROSIVE
8

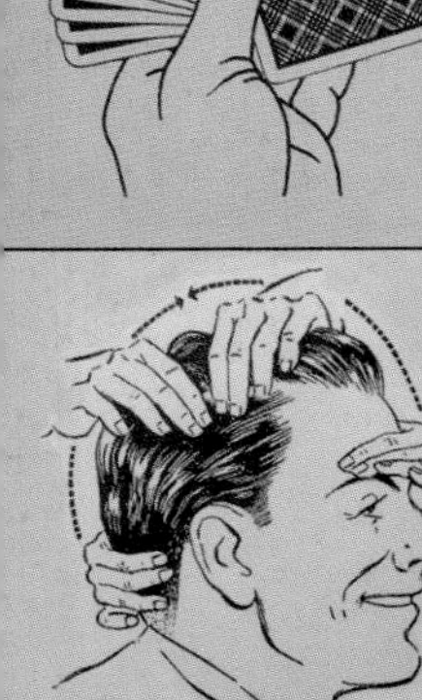

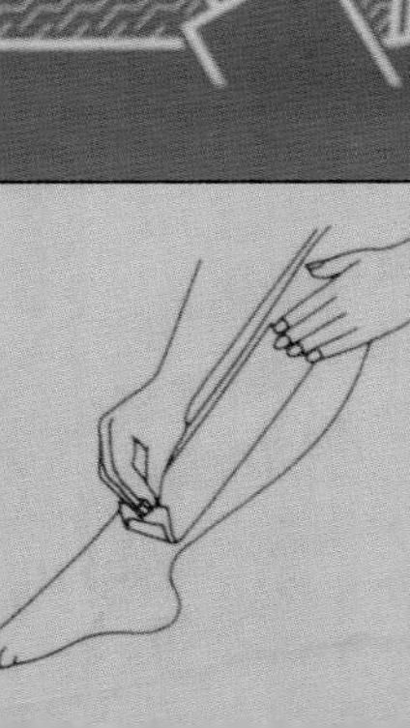

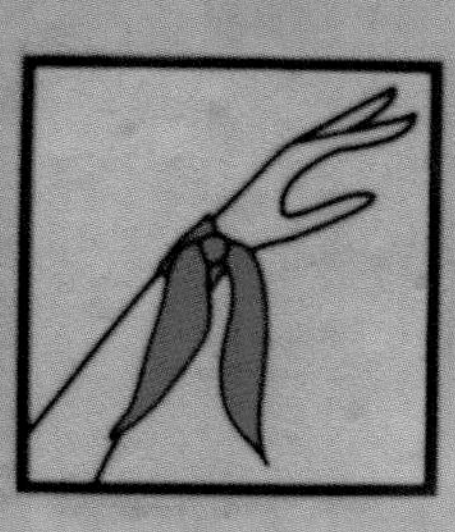

Trinity
Nails

EMPLOYEE RECOGNITION PROGRAM
Nurturing
Spirit Award

ON
OFF
HAND

$
VORSICHT
SOZIALABBAU
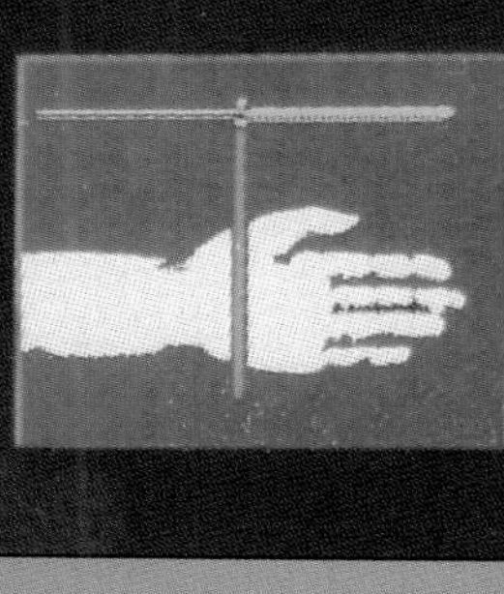

Diverse Hand creams

THE MULTIPLE EXPRESSIONS OF A PRIMARY ICON

JEAN-BENOÎT LÉVY

As individuals we all interpret life through our senses.

However, our personal perceptions do vary according to the diversities and characteristics of the culture in which we have been raised.

As we do have many visual elements of interaction which are used in our culture, we naturally tend to communicate with the most simple signs in order to make ourselves understood.

As a logical result we have reproduced a certain number of symbols understandable by everyone. Hand-signs are one example of a parallel range of non verbal information.

Graphical representations of basic gestures are used in order to augment the effect of our normal written messages.

Used as decorative artifacts or as recurring information, warning or simple instructions, the graphical representations of hand-signs represent our multiple actions, offering a wide range of visual effects in countless styles.

Either represented as clean pictograms, ornamental decorations, effective graphical icons, modern logos or complex symbols, they direct us, expressing simple usability, clarity, inviting us to follow them, leading us toward a direction, expressing a warning, sometimes even giving us an order.

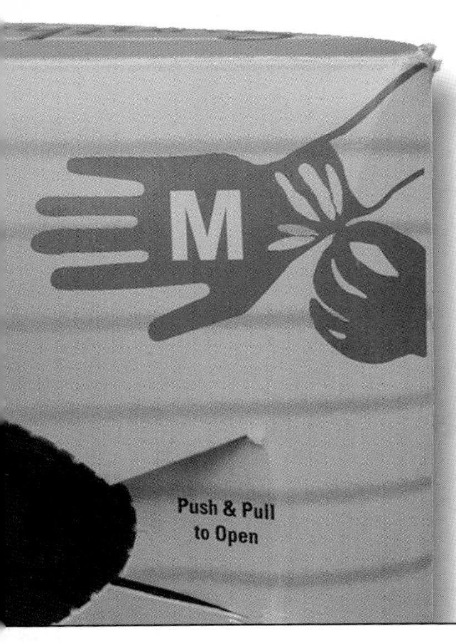
M
Push & Pull
to Open
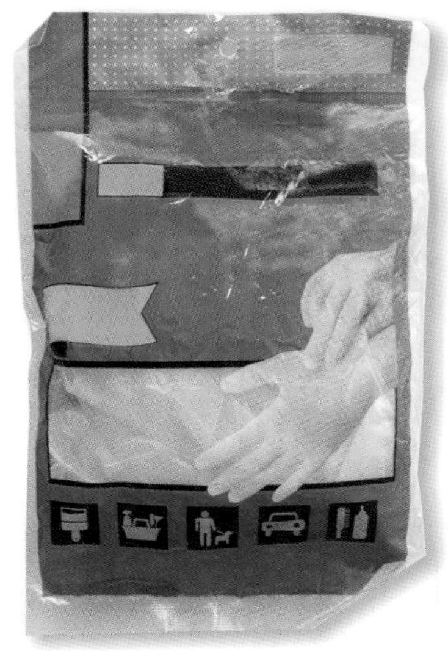

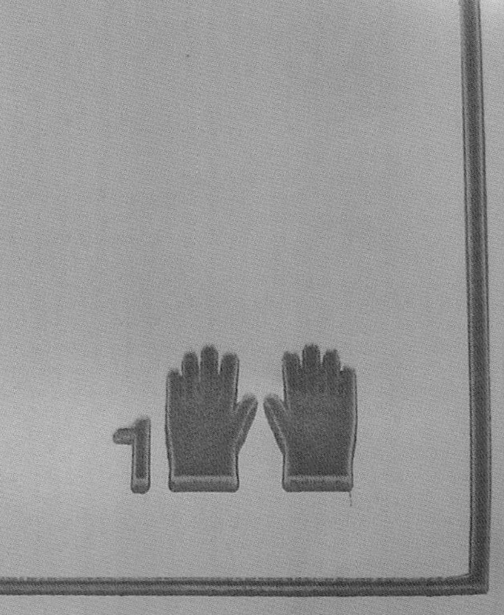
1

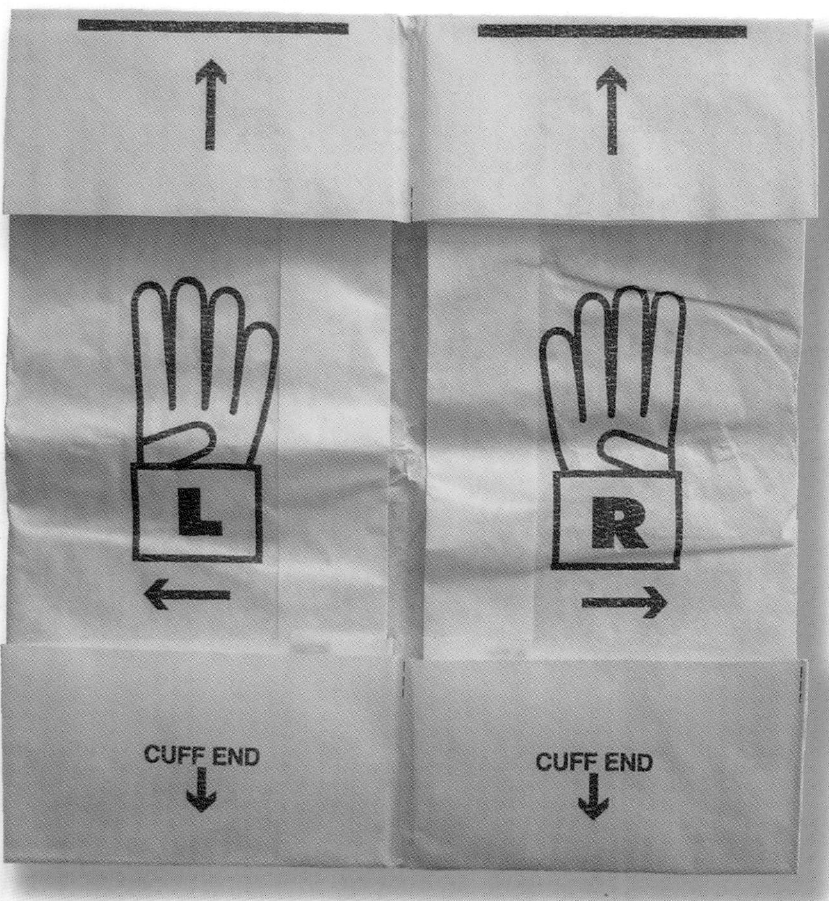

Medical gloves for operations

Illustrative or abstract, stylized or realistic, hand-signs can be informative or simply decorative. Through their shape, their color or their form they can express multiple feelings, transmitting to us a certain way of understanding. Their visual appearance can reinforce any written message.

We look at those signs so often that we take them for granted. Do we really see them? How are we aware of their presence? For any possible product the role of visual styles on packaging is to transmit an external reflection of its content.

Imagine that one tries to erase all the written information on certain packagings which contain illustrations of hands. Just by looking at it, without any surrounding word, the message still stays somehow understandable as the graphic design takes over the text part.

Colorful or black and white, drawn by hand or constructed on computer, outlined or with shadow, bold or thin, complex or simple, their style and esthetic are just like any language: securing or functional, inviting or obliging, subtle or loud, charming or forcing, directing or ordering; those signs are the mirror of our actions and the way we interact. And no matter where we are on the planet, they are everywhere around us in our daily life. As they relate to one of the most important parts of our body, the hand, those visual codes speak to us.

Multinational dish liquid

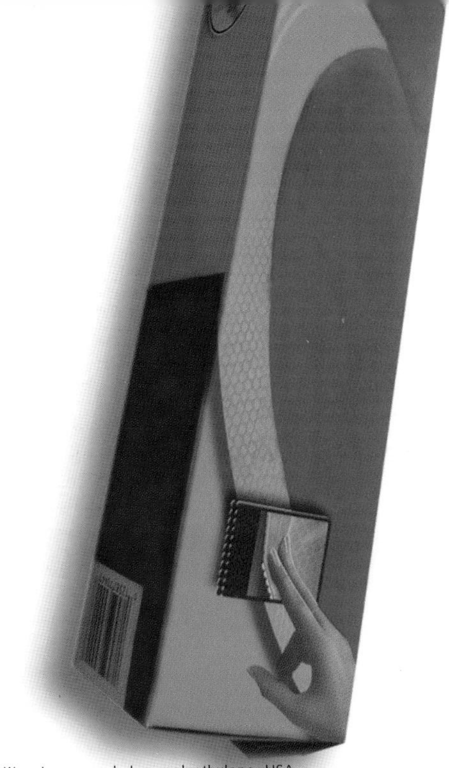

Wraping crysral clear polyethylene, USA

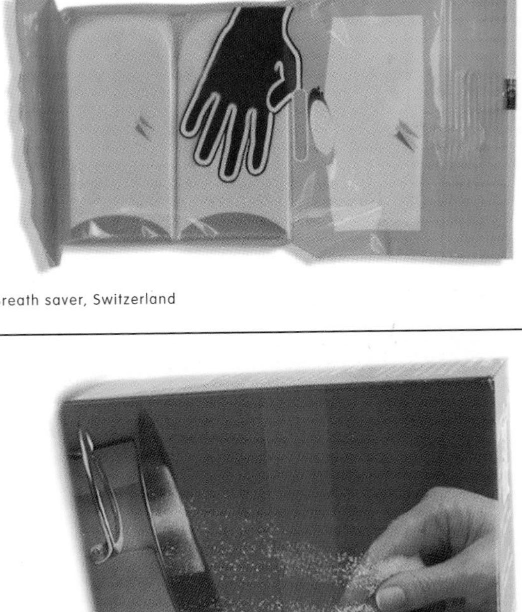

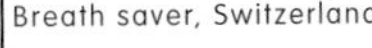

Breath saver, Switzerland

Table salt, Switzerland

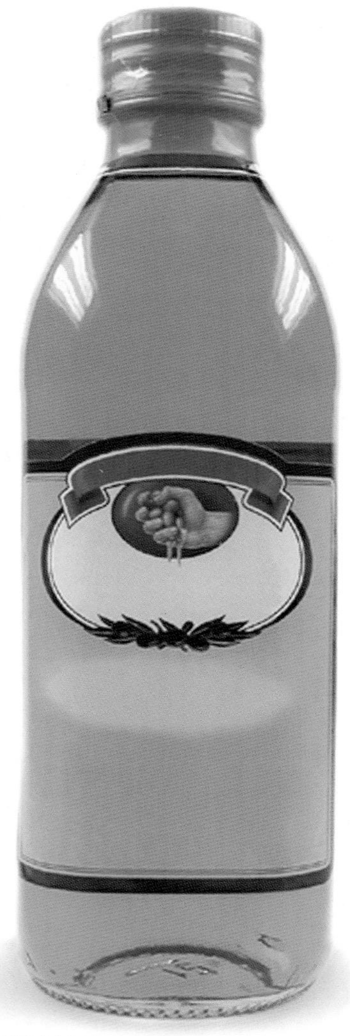

Italian oilve oil

KINDERGARTEN TEST CHART

20/200	200 FT./61 M
20/100	100 FT./30.5M
20/70	70 FT./21.7M
20/50	50 FT./15.2M
20/40	40 FT./12.2M
20/30	30 FT./9.1M
20/20	20 FT./6.1M
20/10	10 FT./3.05M

Kindergarten optical test chart

Universally understandable hand-signs are used to express some of our most basic information needs. Each time we take action, no matter when or where, during the day or at night, at work or in our free time, from the moment we are awake either by leaning or standing, washing, dressing, eating or cleaning, in motion, driving or walking, being passive or active, our eyes encounter those specific icons.

Accompanying us in our actions, explaining how to use our hands, showing us almost how to behave. By their presence, they lead us toward a feeling of independence. At the same time they develop a relation of dependent consumer.

How to open a tube of cream, unfold the top of a container of milk, use any kind of machine, hold a tool, push a button, press and push a door handle, spray wash-powder, handle a razor, swipe a credit card or tear the envelope of a condom, as multiple as our cultures, traditions, languages and ways of expression are, no matter where we are coming from the process of the message functions relatively simply.

Hand-signs can express complexity as they can improve simplicity in our daily life. Crossing over the multiple barriers formed by the countless national languages, the use of those modern hieroglyphs remains as effective for communicating now as it was prior to the development of speech.

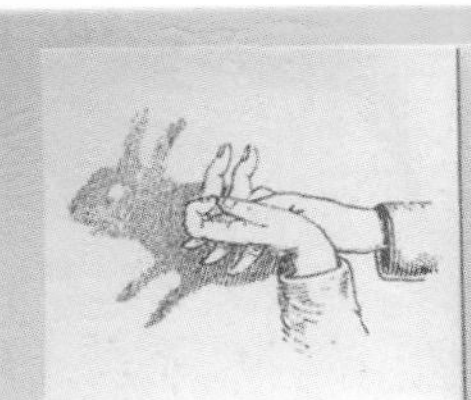

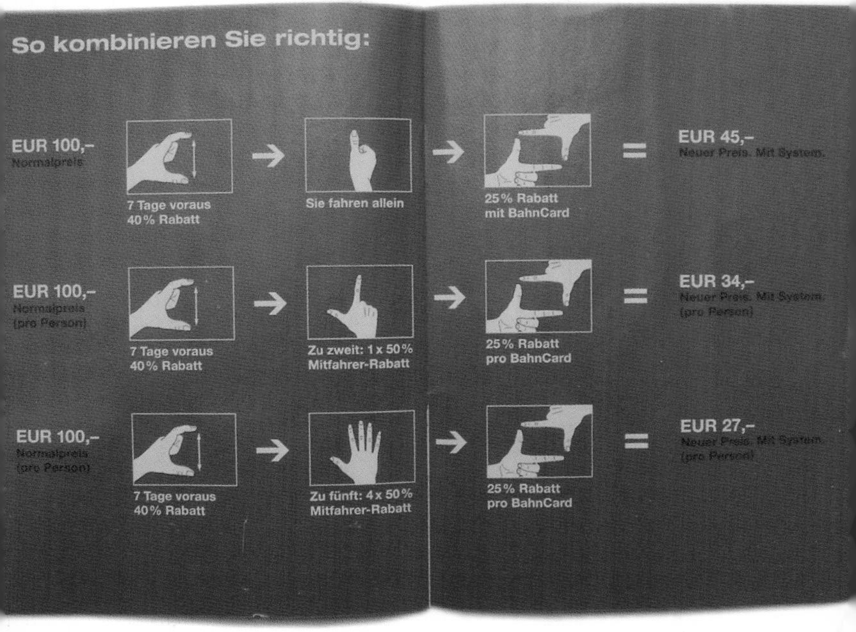

So kombinieren Sie richtig:

EUR 100,–
Normalpreis

7 Tage voraus
40 % Rabatt

Sie fahren allein

25 % Rabatt
mit BahnCard

= EUR 45,–
Neuer Preis. Mit System.

EUR 100,–
Normalpreis
(pro Person)

7 Tage voraus
40 % Rabatt

Zu zweit: 1 x 50 %
Mitfahrer-Rabatt

25 % Rabatt
pro BahnCard

= EUR 34,–
Neuer Preis. Mit System.
(pro Person)

EUR 100,–
Normalpreis
(pro Person)

7 Tage voraus
40 % Rabatt

Zu fünft: 4 x 50 %
Mitfahrer-Rabatt

25 % Rabatt
pro BahnCard

= EUR 27,–
Neuer Preis. Mit System.
(pro Person)

Printed representations of hand-sign systems for communication, advertising or leisure.

Hands

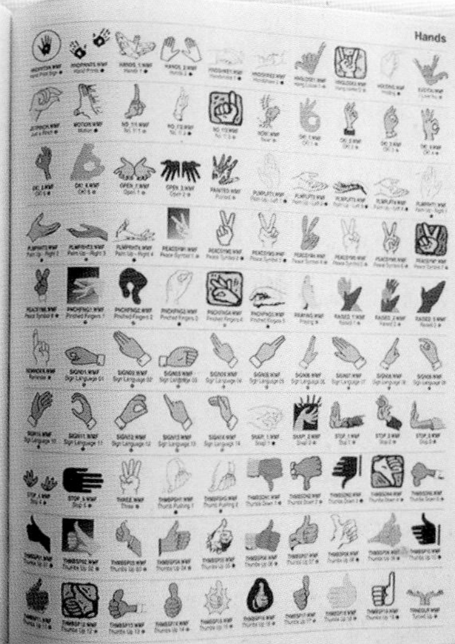
Hands

Hello!
I AM A
DEAF PERSON
I am selling this
Deaf
Education System
card to make my living.
WILL YOU KINDLY BUY ONE
PAY ANY PRICE YOU WISH!
THANK YOU
(over)

American Single-Hand
Manual Alphabet for the Deaf

Hand alphabet used by the Deaf throughout the world. Easy to learn.

GOOD
BAD
PERFECT
CHANCE
FRIEND
O.K.
RIGHT
NO GOOD
GIRL
THANKS
BOY
MARRY

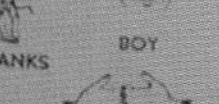
SWEETHEART

THANKS

GOOD LUCK

16

grazioso
dim.

BIBLIOGRAPHY & SOURCES

Greifen und Griffe / Otl Aicher + Robert Kuhn / 1987 / 1995
ISBN 3-88375-061-1 / FSB - Franz Schneider Brakel / Brakel / Germany / www.fsb.de

Hands / John Napier / Revised by Russel H. Tuttle / 1980 / 1993 / ISBN 0-691-02547-9
Princeton University Press / Princeton – New Jersey / www.pupress.princeton.edu

The Hand / Frank R. Wilson / 1998
ISBN 0-679-74047-3 / Vintage Books / New York / USA / www.vintagebooks.com

The Hand - La Mano / Exhibition / Gabriela Rodriguez

Das Hand-Buch / Maria Calderon / Advanced Class for Graphic Design / 1996
Schule für Gestaltung Basel / Fachbibliothek / Basel / Switzerland / www.sfgbasel.ch

Die Hieroglyphen von Heute / Hans-Rudolf Lutz / 1997
Verlag Hans-Rudolf Lutz / Zürich / Switzerland / www.lutz.to

La main – essentiellement / Jean Brun / 1998
ISBN 209-754 152-6 / Nathan / Delpire / Paris / France / www.nathan.fr

Mudras – Geheimsprache der Yogis / Ingrid Ramm-Bonwitt / 1987
Verlag Hermann Bauer KG, Freiburg im Brisgau / Germany / www.frickverlag.de/bauer

Signs, Symbols and Ciphers / Georges Jean / 1998
ISBN 0-8109-2842-6 / Discoveries – Abrams / New York / www.hnabooks.com

Speak Italian – The Fine Art of the Gesture / Bruno Munari / 2005
ISBN 0811847748 / Chronicle Books, San Francisco / www.chroniclebooks.com

Hand Zeichen Sprachen / Klara Jahn / 1996
TM / RSI / 4 - 5 / 1996 / Printing and Paper Union of Switzerland

Die Verschriftung der Gebärdensprache / Beiträge zur Sinographie / Conny Löffler
2004 / ISBN 3-933629-13-6 / SIGNA 7 / Grimma / Germany / www.signographie.de
Verlag Denkmalschmiede Höfgen / Edition Wächterpappel

Kaleideoscope / Die Hand / Yvan Dalain / Swiss Television / Zurich / 1975

BIOGRAPHY

Jean-Benoît Lévy / Multi-task graphic designer. Visual consultant with nomadic aspirations. Born: 1959 in Switzerland. Education at the Basel School of Design (1978-1983) where he was trained under some great names of Swiss typography. J-B L opens his own studio in Basel in 1989 called A N D. For the next 25 years, the A N D team created graphic design for numerous local, regional & national companies & organizations in Switzerland, collaborating when needed with marketing and advertising agencies. Logos / CI / Bookdesign / Advertising Posters / Postage stamps / Signs Systems / Awards and exhibitions in Europe, Japan, USA. Worldwide teaching activities since 1991. Member of AGI since 1998. Lives in San Francisco.

From the same author / H-AND-S / www.myfonts.com/?refby=and
Live / Love postcards & journals / www.chroniclebooks.com
Soda magazine / Nr. 17 / Luxus / www.soda.ch

www.and.ch